I Will Restore You
In Faith, In Hope, In Love

Volume III

I Will Restore You
In Faith, In Hope, In Love

Volume III

Queenship
PUBLISHING COMPANY
P.O. Box 42028 Santa Barbara, CA 93140-2028
(800) 647-9882 • (805) 957-4893 • Fax: (805) 957-1631

© 1999 Queenship Publishing

Library of Congress #: 97-65315

Published by:
    Queenship Publishing
    P.O. Box 42028
    Santa Barbara, CA 93140-2028
    (800) 647-9882 • (805) 957-4893 • Fax: (805) 957-1631

Printed in the United States of America

ISBN: 1-57918-110-4

Declaration

The decree of the Congregation for the Propagation of the **Faith, A.A.S.58, 1186** (approved by Pope Paul VI on October 14, 1966), states that the **Nihil Obstat** and **Imprimatur** are no longer required on publications that deal with private revelations, provided they contain nothing contrary to faith and morals.

The author and publisher wish to manifest their unconditional submission to the final and official judgement of the Magisterium of the Church.

His Holiness, Pope Urban VII states:

"In cases which concern private revelations, it is better to believe than to not believe, for if you believe, and it is proven true, you will be happy that you have believed, because our Holy Mother asked it. If you believe, and it should be proven false, you will receive all blessings as if it had been true, because you believed it to be true." (Pope Urban III, 1623-44)

The Catechism of the Catholic Church states:

Pg.23, #67: "Throughout the ages, there has been so-called "private revelations", some of which have been recognized by the authority of the Church. They do not belong, however, to the deposit of faith. It is not their role to improve or complete Christ's definitive Revelation, but to *help live more fully* by it in a certain period of history. Guided by the magisterium of the Church, the sensus fidelium knows how to discern and welcome in these revelations whatever constitutes an authentic call of Christ or His saints to the Church."

Scripture states:

"Do not quench the Spirit. Do not despise prophetic utterances. Test everything: retain what is good." (1 Thes. 5:19)

Dedication

Dedicated to the Eternal Father, My Abba

Our Father Who Art in Heaven
Hallowed Be Thy Name
Thy Kingdom Come
Thy Will Be Done
On Earth
As It Is In Heaven
Give Us This day
Our Daily Bread
And Forgive Us Our Trespasses
As We Forgive Those Who Trespass Against Us
And Lead Us Not Into Temptation
But Deliver Us From Evil. Amen.

Contents

Acknowledgements

Deepest gratitude to my family for your patience and support, sacrifice and love. My husband and children, you have yet to realize how much you are a part of this work. You are so precious to me.

I acknowledge the prayer group, the United Hearts of Jesus and Mary, for being a great source of strength and encouragement. I am most appreciative of your gifts of the Holy Spirit, discernment, and willingness to intercede and suffer for this work. I cannot thank you enough.

A special acknowledgement to M.H. for so diligently preparing the manuscript for publication. It is a joy to work with you! May God bless you and your beautiful family for the sacrifice of your time and talents. I am most appreciative.

Again, I thank Neal Hughes for the donation and execution of the inspiring cover image. May God contine to use your talents for His Glory.

A debt of gratitude is due to Queenship Publishing, Bob and Claire and the family of Queenship. Your ministry is vital for the Church. Thank you for your support, sacrifice, guidance, and friendship. May God continue to use you to nourish His people!

Finally, thank you, Father Ignatius! You are at the heart of this work through your priestly intercession. Without your discernment and spiritual guidance it would not come to fruition. Your priestly support for my family has kept us going. Only a few realize the tremendous spiritual battle that is involved to bring this volume to the Church and world.

All Glory be to God, the Father, Son, and Holy Spirit now and forever. May Mary, the daughter of the Father, the Mother of the Son and Spouse of the Holy Spirit be with you. Amen.

Foreword

By Fr. Ignatius, S.T.L., S.S.L., Spiritual Director

It is with joy that I am writing a Foreword to Volume Three of the messages and teachings that are present in this book. The beauty of the writings and their richness of spirituality are the product of God's graces acting with greater power in an instrument that has become ever more sensitive and open to the Breath of the Holy Spirit. A life lived in prayer, in the Holy Spirit, and yet filled with daily suffering, has given to this volume a continued journey in the way of the cross, exemplifying a life lived in obedience and surrender to the Lord and His Will.

The beauty of the messages and teaching must always be seen in the light of Jesus' desire for souls to "alleviate His Thirst". In the message of 10-24-96, we read a passage that gives both the relationship of a soul's journey before the Lord and the salvific goal for others and the world itself. In response to Jesus' question, **Will you gather souls to alleviate My Thirst?** The messenger will ask, "How, Lord?"

The following quote, I think, captures the essence of this book. Jesus replied: **Do whatever I tell you; go wherever I send you. Suffer silently. Permit Me to use you whenever I ask; wait prayerfully, patiently, for My Command. Do everything with Me and realize always, we are together as One Heart of Love. Do you understand now, your thirst is My Own? First, I caused you to thirst for Me. Now, I cause you to thirst for souls because you are with Me and in Me. You love with My own limitless Love because you exist inside My Heart of Infinite Love. My Thirst continues.**

Do these words apply only to the messenger? No. They reflect the undying love that Jesus places in a soul for Him and all those whom He loves. To read this book does bring joy into one's heart. Yet underneath its beauty is a call to the reader to reflect and respond in the deepest level of one's graced person to the demands of the all-consuming love of the Lord.

Volume I portrayed an almost romantic type of love where the Lord captured the soul. Volumes II and III brought in the Cross and an appeal to love Him on the Cross and unite one's heart and soul in Him as He offers up this gift of Himself to the Father for us all.

I must confess that my relationship with the messenger has been a growth process for me. In what way? The messages and spirituality we see in the book come from a person living an "ordinary life" of a mother and wife: raucous music of two sons, family difficulties, business problems, extended family problems, etc. No one knows what is taking place in her life that appears so "normal", yet has within it on a daily basis an enormous love of the Lord and surrender to His Will. She does not speak of these graces in her soul except to give me an account of them. And bearing witness to what takes place in these writings has enriched my own faith, hope, and love.

To read this book is to understand that we are called into a deep personal surrender of ourselves to the Lord. We are all called to holiness as we read in the Vatican document *Lumen Gentium* (Dogmatic Constitution of the Church, Ch. 5). This universal call from the Church is beautifully supplemented by the personal, intimate surrender of the self, seen in this book. Without this personal love, there will be no response to the Church's appeal.

The only fear that this book could engender is the one we are all subject to, namely, a deeper personal surrender to the Lord and His Will. As a book of teachings in our day, with all its confusion, chaos, and flight from God, the reader is uplifted and supported to "fight the good fight" and cling tightly to the Lord and His Blessed Mother. That the world is in crisis and the Church is suffering within and without is before us all.

In his own day Paul, inspired by the Holy Spirit, will write, "Our struggle is not with flesh and blood, but with the principalities, with the powers, with the world rulers of this present darkness, with the evil spirits in the heavens." (Eph. 6:12) Certainly, these words describe the spiritual warfare present in our age. However, we need not feel helpless or paralyzed. We need not fear. The "Do Not Fear" that we see in the gospel, repeated by Pope John

Paul II in the beginning of his pontificate, is repeated in this book again and again.

The very existence of these messages and teachings bring before us the love of Our Lord and His Mother. Meditations on these writings can only increase our courage to fight the enemy of the Lord who is our enemy. They speak of the love for Jesus in the Eucharist, daily prayer, a true commitment to work for the Lord in His Church, the role of family as domestic church.

The growing spirituality that we see in the laity of our day but illumines the words of St. Paul, "where sin abounds grace abounds the more." The recognition of this reality is evidenced in the letters received from the hierarchy and laity who have read the previous volumes. A priest wrote: "Reading *I Will Restore You* has had a powerful effect on me and my spiritual life. It's as though the books were written just for me – their power and unction." The universality of the books' message is touching hearts in many countries, (eg. Canada, Australia, Italy, Sweden). I hope and pray that this will continue to move hearts throughout the nations.

There is no doubt that it is providential that this book is published on the eve of the millennium. Our present Holy Father, John Paul II, speaks of a springtime for the Church as she enters the new millennium. He writes in *Mission of the Redeemer*, — "As the third millennium of the redemption draws near, God is preparing a great springtime for Christianity and we can already see its first signs..."

May this work, graced in its origin and completion be for you, the reader, the instrument that the Holy Spirit uses to bring you into a greater love for Jesus and the Father. And may you have greater awareness of the maternal mediation of the Blessed Virgin Mary and intercession of the Communion of Saints. In the tradition of the Church, throughout history, the Lord has raised up those to inflame and strengthen hearts in a time of crisis. May these writings do this for you.

I leave you with the words of St. Paul (Eph. 4:11-16):

"And He gave some as apostles, others as prophets, others as evangelists, others as pastors and teachers, to equip the holy ones for the work of ministry, for the building up of the Body of Christ, until we all attain to the unity of faith and knowledge of the Son of God, to mature manhood, to the extent of the full stature of Christ, so that we may no longer be infants tossed by waves and swept along by trickery, from their cunning in the interests of deceitful scheming.

Rather, living the Truth in Love, we should grow in every way into Him who is the Head, Christ, from whom the whole body, joined and held together by every supporting ligament, with the proper functioning of each part, brings about the body's growth and builds itself up in Love."

Explanation of the Cover of the Book

On October 9, 1996, while praying the Rosary with my spiritual director, the following vision was received and Jesus asked that an image be drawn depicting the vision. Jesus also led me to the artist who would draw the image for the cover in fulfillment of His request.

During Father's meditation the Resurrection decade of the Rosary, suddenly I received a vision of St. Peter's Basilica in Rome. It was being raised up toward the heavens for all on earth to see. It had been thoroughly purified and made radiantly beautiful becoming a treasury attracting the whole world. The Light of the Holy Spirit overflowed the Mystical Bride of Christ and radiated outward through the windows and doors, which were wide open. From within, the Holy Spirit radiated out to the entire world, all people, and all nations.

Then the scene changed to the interior main altar of St. Peter's Basilica. The Dove of the Holy Spirit had wrapped His wings around a beautiful Gold Monstrance containing the Eucharistic Jesus. This was a gesture signifying the Spirit's protection of the True Presence of Jesus upon the altar. When the time arrived ordained by the Father, the Holy Spirit opened His Wings fully to reveal the glory of the Eucharistic Jesus present upon the altar. Brilliant light rays burst forth from the Blessed Sacrament and the Holy Spirit and all of creation received the grace of restoration in Faith, Hope, and Love.

On October 14, 1996, in prayer Jesus indicated that the cover image should depict the Immaculate Heart of Mary, her pierced heart near the Blessed Sacrament and within the altar area of St. Peter's signifying her maternal mediation.

Messages

1. **7-18-96** Rosary with Father at my home.
Intercede Toward a New Pentecost

After the decade of the Descent of the Holy Spirit, Our Lady said: *Dear little ones, pray in joyful expectation of the new outpouring of the Holy Spirit on earth. Gather together in the upper room of my Immaculate Heart and from this house of prayer, this fortified city, let us cry out fervently to the Eternal Father saying as one voice, "Now is the time, Father, Abba, let there be a New Pentecost! Come Holy Spirit and renew the face of the earth! Send the fire of Your Divine Love and transform the darkness of this age into the light of a new era of unity, peace, and love!*

I come into your midst, dear children, to call you to my Immaculate Heart so that from within we can be one cenacle of continuous prayer for the salvation of the world. Many find yourselves with me, with Rosaries in hand, crying out for a new day! Please continue to lift up your hearts to our Triune God, interceding for mercy and justice toward new life and grace, a new Pentecost on earth!

You, who are gathered in my Immaculate Heart, form the cenacles that form the army that battles the sin of the world.

It is urgent that we pray together unceasingly, offering every sacrifice, all sufferings toward a civilization of Love, because daily, I am made to observe many souls fall into the abyss of hell. I cannot bear to lose even one soul without my maternal heart being pierced with great pain. And when the sword pierces me for each lost soul, the sword of suffering touches you also because you are in my heart. We suffer every loss together. Just as we rejoice in every victory over sin together!

Because Satan does not rest, but feverishly carries off as many souls as possible, I must ask you who are within my Immaculate

Heart to offer more sacrifices of love and more prayers. In reparation for the rampant sin of the world, I must ask for more intercession from you, which draws more grace and mercy for sinners.

Let us continue to pray fervently, for the grace of a New Pentecost on earth. The Holy Spirit shall come with His fire and ignite the earth with Divine Love, burning away evil and leaving you in True Light. Until this precious moment comes, stay with me, gathered in the upper room of my Immaculate Heart and pray, in unity and in peace. I love you. Thank you, dear children, for listening to me. I am your Mother.

2. **7-26-96** Prayer Group
Know Yourself and Depend on God

Dear little ones,

I bless you in the name of the Most Holy Trinity who permits me to be with you in this special way. By means of your consecration, each one is like a beautiful flower in the garden of my Immaculate Heart. It is the variety, which enhances the beauty of the garden, which grows to glorify God.

You are becoming more aware of your weaknesses, incapacities, and spiritual poverty. This is a great gift from God. The more you know yourself, the more you depend upon the strength of God who can supply His own strength and riches. Depend more on God and do not be afraid of this. It is prideful to be self-sufficient. Depend on the Supplier of all good things and realize without Him there is no goodness!

He is revealing your neediness and weakness because you have prayed for the truth of self-knowledge. This is vitally important in the spiritual life, in the living of the Truth. He permits you to have many interior struggles causing you to choose Him repeatedly and to forfeit your former ways of the world.

It is a gift to be hidden and needy, always depending on God from one moment to the next. Such are the children of God. And these are blessed most abundantly by Him. To the most unlikely, humble and pure of heart, He gives the most important missions on earth. Do not be impatient with yourselves or the members of your families or prayer group. Be humble and desire nothing more than to be humble and hidden, faithful in your duties and vigilant of your heart. May it belong to God first. May you never harbor anything within, which is unworthy of Him.

Dear children, let God be the Master and do not think that you know better than He! Many people approach Him in prayer with such a disposition. This is foolish! Many people pray for lofty or extraordinary things in the spiritual life. This is prideful and must be avoided. Ask only for His Will and the cross! Humiliations and persecutions are the crosses that raise your soul to sanctity in God's eyes. The world will think you foolish to pray or sacrifice or long for union with God. But these are the ways of true wisdom and union with God is your fulfillment and joy.

Do not become frustrated because you are weak or needy. Embrace your incapacity and fill yourself with His infinite capacity. Rejoice because God has drawn close to you and you are alive in His Heart of Love. You must decrease and He must increase. I love you and will continue to help form you for God. Thank you for your prayers. I am your Mother.

3. 7-30-96
Purification Leading to Sanctification

At the end of the Rosary with Father, I heard: **My creation, Too many are presently under the influence of darkness because of the pride of self-sufficiency, independence, and rebellion. Evil has penetrated even into the areas of society which are meant to be sacred treasuries of True Goodness. In My Mercy, I will enter where the darkness has gone and make clean what belongs to Me.**

The necessary purification will progress rapidly. Mankind will be humbled so as to receive the Truth again. The Holy Spirit goes before Me to prepare the hearts of My people. Soon there will be a new fire on earth; the fire that purifies and transfigures the hearts of mankind. I will manifest My Presence to lead you into an era of sanctification. The world will live in accordance with the Father's Divine Will. Evil will lose its power over you because I intend to expose it to the fullness of My

Light. I will manifest My Presence to lead you back to the Eternal Father so that He is glorified in His Creation. Be reconciled and keep watch.

You have spent enough time in the deception of the liar and the thief who has led you away from the Truth and robbed you of True Love and Peace.

The converted heart of man will live in the fullness of grace. Humanity shall know the Heart of their Redeemer! In the knowledge of My True Love you will freely choose to live My Law of Love. That will be your peace. The earth will radiate new life having been purged of the evil, which has been allowed to test the hearts of mankind for the past century.

During the purification, there will be disasters of various types and innocent victims. But the innocent ones will receive a martyr's crown. The disasters are a form of purification brought about through man's acceptance of evil. Your idols will be exposed and crushed.

I have chosen this generation to be a witness of My Omnipotence because I will reach into the depths of your darkness and bring a great good out of it! Then you will know that I am your Deliverer!

The prayers of fervent and victim souls hasten the days of purification. You who have reconciled with Me must pray fervently for your families, churches, nations, so that by your heartfelt prayers, they are freed from the clutches of the evil one.

Pray especially that the pride of the human heart will be turned into humility. The humble are the wise ones who serve Me first. But the world calls you fools and you will be persecuted even by your own families, friends, and co-workers. There will be much to suffer toward the sanctification of mankind. Out of the chaos and confusion of your age, I will bring about the sanctification of the human heart. I am your Jesus.

4. **7-31-96** Rosary with Father
The Pope Who Will Proclaim the Whole Truth About Mary

At the Fifth Glorious Mystery, Jesus said: **The coronation of Mary Most Holy, Mother of All, Queen of Heaven and Earth,** is not fully realized by mankind. Her co-redemption of souls, her mediation of all graces, the truth that she is your advocate, is not yet fully realized by mankind.

My people, the whole truth about Mary is a jewel not only for her crown but also for your lives on earth. Pray fervently for My Vicar, My Peter of today. Pray that soon he will complete the coronation of Our Mother. It is fitting that Pope John Paul II, the great light of this age, be the one to proclaim to the world the entire truth about Mary.

The graces which will flow from the papal definition of the whole truth about our Mother are most needed for this generation and those to come! Already a part of the Church's treasury of Truth and Tradition, it is hidden and must be lifted up for all to behold, to know in your hearts. All of our children require the fullness of her maternal love.

What will be divided will be divided. But more will come together and remain together, full of new grace. My family will be unified when our Mother is accepted in the roles she has faithfully fulfilled since receiving My words at the foot of the cross, "Woman, behold your Son!"

This Pope, prepared from the beginning, has been the one chosen to be My Hand in the completion of the coronation of our Mother. But his hands are not totally free. There are many against him. Pray for the cardinals and bishops and priests who surround him. The Immaculate Heart of Mary will lead him to fulfill this task, his mission, at the Father's appointed time. But many sacrifices and prayers are needed to free his hands at the appointed time, which is soon.

Pray very much for our Pope! You do not comprehend the Light that he is for all the world, not only the Roman Catholic Church! He is My Advocate for True Life in a world which daily embraces more death. All on earth owe this holy instrument of Mine a great debt of gratitude because he has procured for you inestimable graces. I cannot refuse his humble heart so infused with the fire of Divine Charity! Pray for him and his office. Both are threatened by the evil one. He intercedes for mankind and becomes a victim for all. He embraces all suffering while courageously awaiting a new springtime for humanity. My favor is upon him and his courageous "Fiat to the Divine Will" is the catalyst for the salvation of many souls who would otherwise perish.

It is toward the salvation of souls that he will proclaim the whole truth about our Mother, completing the coronation of Mary Most Holy. And her Immaculate Heart will gather in My family of man, and become the doorway to the reign of My Eucharistic Love on earth. She is My gift to you. And all of heaven awaits your acknowledgement of such a magnificent masterpiece! You who are awake, pray unceasingly for this grace and I will bless you with fuller understanding of her maternal roles. I am your Jesus.

5. 8-7-96
More Spiritual Warfare and Power of Intercession

During the Rosary with Father at my home, I received an image of the United States flag torn in half by legions of evil spirits. Then I saw the flags of many European countries and South American countries being torn in half as well. Over all of this was the word "division."

Then I saw my heart in Mary's hands and she was giving it to Jesus. Then she seemingly put Jesus' heart inside of me to replace my own. Immediately, arrows from many devils assailed my heart. Mary said: *The real target of the enemy is my Son, Jesus, and it is His Heart in you that makes you another target for Satan. Be vigilant and discern the spirits!"*

Then I saw my tears falling onto dry desert land. After a while, from the watering of tears, the land turned green, fertile, and beautiful. Mother Mary said: *Child, your tears are not wasted! The tears of victim souls water the parched ones and cause new life to grow out of nothingness.*

Then I saw the Heart of Jesus! It was large enough to contain all of creation! Our Lady said: *No one is outside His Love!*

Then I received an image of Jesus on the cross. His side was pierced and gushing water and blood. Our Lady collected His Precious Blood and Water in a chalice. Then she offered the cup to me and I drank from it. As I drank, an angel came and pierced my heart. I heard, "Open up your heart and give life to others. Imitate the Lord."

The last image that I recall was an angel of consolation who ministered to Father and presented him with a mystical white lily. I heard: "This is a symbol of your victory over many devils. I bring you God's peaceful strength. You are battling many demons and you are winning by the power of the Holy Spirit in you." With that, the angel departed.

6. 8-8-96
The Division of Countries and Warning to the USA

After the Rosary, Our Lady said: *Dear children, the devil seeks to divide countries.* (She is referring to the image of the various country flags being torn apart.) *By dividing he can conquer a country, a church, a family, a person. Be aware of division! You will see it all around you. The more divided you are as persons, families, churches, or countries, the weaker you are and your defense against evil forces is diminished.*

When Jesus was among you on earth, He said, **I come to divide.** *Dear children, He divides good from evil, Truth from falsehood. He divides by making a distinction between right and wrong. But Satan divides without distinction. He divides what is good, and he will divide what should not be divided.*

Dear children, remember that Satan seeks to destroy or steal what belongs to God. Think of your own heart. Is it unified in the Holy Spirit or divided between yourself, the world and God? Division begins in the heart and spreads like a cancer until you become a divisive instrument.

Live God's law of Love and do not divide by judging one another. Be careful that your own self-righteousness does not divide you from people. Like my Son, Jesus, make the distinction between truth and falsehood but always love without distinction! This is difficult in your human nature, but you must strive to live it.

Entire nations are being assailed by the high powered evil spirit of division. Your own country (The United States) will grow weaker because of division in government and among people. The ruling power in your country is pride and it is always divisive and self-seeking. There will be many victims of the false power of pride in your country.

Dear children, turn back to God! You must pray as a country and unify under God. If you do not turn back as a country, then the enemy will continue to divide and conquer you in various evil ways. These various attacks will dishearten the nation and set the stage for diminishing its power and influence. Your freedoms will be threatened.

You are not able to unify yourselves except through faith in God, prayer and reparation. The pride of self-sufficiency will make you weak. Without God, if you continue to reject my Son and make money your god, then your country will suffer and evildoers will take control over many aspects of your lives. Heed my words, dear children. I am trying to help you. I love you and your country. Your Mother.

7. **9-11-96** Rosary with Father at my home.
Victory: Mine, The Church , and Yours

At the first Glorious Mystery, after Father's meditation on the Resurrection, I received the image of Jesus as the King of Glory, all dazzling white light and "victory" was somehow manifested in and through Him.

He said: **My people, do not forget that I am victorious over all! There is nothing that can prevail over My Omnipotence! I am Love and you who are My Own are begotten of Love.**

As Satan has released his legions to tempt the entire world, I shall strengthen you with new Divine Graces. You will have new energy that comes from My Divine Love. My grace will sustain you and you also will be victorious. My Love is the fire within your hearts, the fire for Good. Burn brightly with love for one another and strengthen the weak and weary. You are the light of the world and I act through you to overcome the sin of the world. There is only a remnant of true believers who have not forsaken the faith and who live to love and serve Me. You are the ones who will call down from heaven the New

Jerusalem, My victorious Bride. My Church, My Mystical Body, shall be full of My glory made manifest as never before.

The purification shall make everything clean. My Church shall become a welcome beacon drawing people to her in a renewed light. And those who come will be filled because she will be restored to a House of Prayer. And this will happen through the Triumph of the Two Hearts, and through the hearts of you, My faithful victim lambs. To you I have distributed the gifts of the Holy Spirit and you are fortified in every way. You suffer, but not in vain. You sacrifice for the sake of a victory, which is emblazoned in your hearts.

Here I had a vision of the Church as a radiant diamond in the Almighty Hands of the Eternal Father. Jesus made it a gift to the Father and the Father was pleased with His Son and His gift. Then Jesus said: **My people, the boldness of the enemy will not outdo the boldness of the Holy Spirit! The victory is Mine! Remember this always!**

During the decade of the Ascension, Jesus said: **My creation, Look only to Me for all your needs and I will supply all that is best for you! Do not look at yourselves or one another. You are My children and I long to give you what you need. Turn to Me. Too many are looking to themselves for answers and solutions which are found only in Me – through prayer.**

8. **9-11-96 (B)**
The Messages Will be Living Water for a Parched Earth

At the Descent of the Holy Spirit decade, Father prayed that the book of messages would be filled with the Fire of Divine Love and that graces would be given through them to heal His people. When Father finished his prayer, I saw the Blessed Mother, pouring graces from her Immaculate Heart onto the book of messages.

Our Lady said: *Dear children, this work of God will be for many a source of living water in a time when the earth will be very parched and thirsty! It has served an important purpose already and it shall continue to serve to teach and guide people into the era of sanctification.*

Especially in the days of transition, it will become for many, a necessary source of grace to encourage and strengthen people. The message books will guide people during a time of great confusion on earth. During this time, it will be necessary to know that God is with you, always loving you, because your faith will be severely tested. The cost of discipleship will increase and the practice of your faith will bring increasing persecution upon you. Much of what you have taken for granted will not be openly available for you for a period of time.

You must be purified, dear children! You are birthing the triumph of my Immaculate Heart and the reign on my Son's Eucharistic Heart. It is a painful process and takes patient endurance, which comes through prayer. There is much to suffer toward the restoration of faith, hope, and love on earth because the sin of the world increases daily and entire nations are tempting the Hand of God.

Be steadfast in your faith, dear children, and you will not falter. Cling to my Son, Jesus. Cherish one another. Thank you for your prayers and sacrifices. I love you. I am your Mother.

9. **10-1-96** Feast of St. Therese of Lisieux
The Little Flower's Way of Love

In the church following Mass I heard: "Dear child, in the eyes of the world I lived a life of obscurity. However, in the eyes of God, the obscurity of my life took on profound meaning. How is it that the little things mean so much to God? The littlest things become meaningful offerings when wrapped in true love. Our little love is magnified in the Infinite Love of God. His Divine Magnanimity envelops our littleness. Few souls are called to do great things on earth, but all souls are called to great love! Love is the universal calling of each and every soul! Love is a decision coming from the human will infused with God's grace. Everyone is capable of love because God's Own Love is written in the heart of every man. Love Himself makes us capable of love and to love is the way to sainthood – the shortest, surest way to heaven!

Many souls on earth are living lives of obscurity, where in secret, they love God and have charity for souls which draws heavenly graces for the salvation of people who would otherwise never know love. How pleasing this is to God, to all of heaven. And how necessary to save souls!

The heavenly court is at the disposal of those who desire our intercession. We assist souls according to God's Will and their disposition to His grace. Therefore, dear friends, become like a child who opens up to the Father completely, trusting in His Infinite Goodness and expecting everything that he needs!

Pray for an increase in faith because many souls no longer believe in God. Without belief in God, there is a crisis of love without which life is void.

I burn with charity for all souls. Strive to let charity reign in you. Be little and it will be easier to love and be loved. How glorious that God has answered my prayer – I am with Love, loving Him and loving you in Him! I am free to shower roses, a variety of graces, upon souls on earth, and I do so, especially in the Church. O Body of Christ, remember that your heart is Love! Fulfill your mission! I am His little flower." (St. Therese)

10. **10-2-96** Feast of the Guardian Angels
The Gift of Guardian Angels

Following Holy Mass, I received an image of a guardian angel with a sword engaged in battle with a dark angel. The guardian angel was a pure spirit of light while the evil spirit had no light at all. Though both are created spirits, the evil spirit could not have light because it separated itself from the Light, God. The guardian angel had light because it exists before the face of God and is a reflection of the Light it beholds, God. I was amazed to observe the power of the guardian angel and the intensity of the battle. This magnificent created spirit of light, my guardian angel, engages in such spiritual warfare over my soul? Is this not another indication of the dignity of a soul? I was pondering this, when I heard Our Lady speak.

Dear children, On this special feast of the Guardian Angels, I invite you to ponder the gift that has been given to you by God. I invite you to ponder the dignity of your soul before God. Can you recognize God's Love and Mercy for you, soul, in the granting of a special angel to defend and guide you? Consider your guardian angel a great gift from God. Consider that your guardian angel engages in battle over your soul. Especially in this age, when evil has permeated every aspect of your culture, your angel battles constantly to help you to walk the straight and narrow path leading to God. This angel exists in the presence of God always. He is given a command from God to protect you from evil. This protection is vital especially in this age when the devil has released all of the demons from hell to prowl the earth to steal souls from God.

Dear children, too many are blind to evil. Too many are accepting the lie that the devil does not exist. He most certainly exists! It is the truth and the teaching of the Roman Catholic Church from the beginning. Do not take this matter lightly or you will certainly open up yourselves and your families to evil attacks from the one that you refuse to believe exists. Observe the increase of evil everywhere! Your angel is constantly engaged in battle over your soul. You also must engage in the fight against evil. God has given you all the gifts of the Holy Spirit; all the spiritual armor necessary to fight the enemy of your soul. Accept this truth. Pray that you can become a strong spiritual warrior by the power of the Holy Spirit in you. Put on the armor daily (Eph. 6). The enemy never rests. Work with your guardian angel. Your soul has a dignity that is worth fighting for. Protect yourselves with the power of the Spirit. Love is the power and the weapon is faith in God. I love you, your Mother.

11. **10-3-96**
Mass for the Healing of the Family Tree

Father offered Mass for the healing of our family tree, using the format published by Fr. John Hampsch, C.M., P. O. Box 19100, Los Angeles, CA 90019-0100.

When I first heard of such a thing, I was skeptical, though it has been part of the Church's history. In this year of increased spiritual attacks on my family and those close to me, I could see the necessity of offering such a Mass. I know that the enemy exists and targets families in a persistent, divisive way. Many of these evil spirits have been attacking our families for generations and the Mass can break the oppression for many family members.

As soon as Father began the Mass I saw an image of many souls, waist high in flames of fire. Their hands were outstretched to us as they cried out for help. As the Mass continued, I saw them rise out of the flames slowly and they were relieved.

Suddenly, I saw another scene. Our Blessed Mother took our hands and led us to a doorway. She stopped before the doorway and put a veil of protection over us, careful not to open that door without this protective veil. She opened the door to show us a deep realm of evil spirits, which had been part of our respective family trees. I was peering into an utterly dark, cold chamber of evil where souls were held in bondage. I heard hissing and growling noises.

She was showing us that through such a Mass, a door is opened so that evil spirits which have remained in families, hidden but effective, are exposed to the Light: the Body, Blood, Soul and Divinity of Jesus. This dispels their power and souls are set free of oppressive spirits. Through the Mass, we cover all the intergenerational spirits that have targeted our families with the Salvific Blood of the Lamb.

Later, when Father offered the Mass for the healing of the prayer group's respective family trees, at the Sign of Peace, he asked us to mutually forgive any pain we have caused one another. This exercise of mutual forgiveness, was a vital step and healing for us as well as the members of our respective family trees. Any unforgiveness hidden in the heart, blocks healing and increases the oppression. Forgiveness is a grace from God and we must pray for it. Help us, Lord, to forgive one another!

After Holy Communion while Father was seated, I was given the image of his deceased parents standing right before him. It seemed to me that they had come from heaven to thank their son for offering the Mass for the healing of the members of their family tree. There was a beautiful moment of union between Father and his parents.

12. **10-7-96** Feast of Our Lady of the Rosary
The Power of the Rosary

At Holy Communion, I saw Our Lady, St. Michael, and many angels descend from heaven and put Rosaries around the earth making them the means by which they proceeded to lift the globe out of the darkness which surrounded it. Following the image, I had difficulty because I could not fathom that the prayers of the Rosary were that powerful. Immediately, Our Lady corrected me.

Dear children, the Rosary is prayer wrapped around the mysteries of the Gospel, wrapped around the life of my Son. The Gospels are the revelation of God's Infinite Love and the truth of Love Himself. How efficacious to mediate upon the Gospel message of Divine Love contained in the Mysteries of the Rosary! And when you do so, your own hearts are lifted into the infinite spiritual world of God.

The Rosary is prayer and prayer is necessary for your personal sanctity but also for the ongoing redemption of the world. Especially in these days of yours, when all the devils have been released from hell to tempt you away from God, prayer is necessary to overcome temptations and save souls.

Prayer transfigures you into a new creation. The Presence of my Son, Jesus, is made manifest in you who pray because prayer gives way to union with my Son.

Would the Father send me from heaven to earth to give you the gift of the Rosary if it were not important? Blessed are you, little children, who have taken up this prayer and opened your heart to its grace. Whether you perceive it or not, the Rosary is forming you and you are being blessed by it. Even if you are praying the Rosary simply because I have asked you to do this, you are receiving graces.

The Rosary is a weapon against evil. The devils despise it because by the divine Mysteries (of the Rosary), *God redeemed the world. The devil, a liar from the beginning, wants you to forget the mysteries of the Rosary. Without these truths, deeply rooted in your hearts, the devil can lead you to forget them and this can lead to deep discouragement, even despair. The devil wants to lead you into sin which separates you from God and he sets traps all around you. Your earthly pilgrimage is a battle and prayer is a means of combat. You must pray as much as possible because this will give you the spiritual strength you need and enable you to keep your peace of soul when everything around you is in turmoil. Take up your Rosaries and persevere in prayer. Now, more than ever, it is needed for the sake of saving souls. I love you. Your Mother.*

13. **10-9-96**
Sacrifice for the Sake of Love

Following Mass Our Lady said: *Dear ones, you have not yet understood the true meaning of love. The world portrays a false love, which begins and ends with "self." Many of you have settled for this false love. Ego-centered love is a type of bondage and too many are chained by this selfish love.*

God alone is True Love and He is the source of all true love, human and Divine. God must be the center of your heart; the center of your love relationships. If you are to love correctly, you must draw from the one true Source. In His Love, you become forgetful of yourself and learn to sacrifice for the sake of those you love. He alone can teach you to love without distinction in a selfless manner. Dear children, love enough to lay down your lives for one another! This kind of love is found in a human heart, which has been permeated by the Holy Spirit, and you must pray for it!

When I ask you to pray especially the Rosary, I do so because I know how it can penetrate hearts! It cultivates the soil of your heart so as to prepare it for Divine Grace. The way of true love is not easy. Few find it because few seek after it. I pray that one day you will understand the beauty of sacrifice for the sake of love. Please pray with me. I love you. Your Mother

14. **10-9-96 (B)** Rosary with Father at my home.
The Triumph of the Two Hearts

After Father's closing prayers Our Lady said: *Dear children, this time in history has been called the Age of Mary. The Father has permitted me to come to you in many visitations and messages. I invite you to consecrate yourselves to my Immaculate Heart be-*

cause my heart is set on the Divine Will of God. The triumph of my Immaculate Heart will be the triumph of the Sacred Heart because although we have two physical hearts, we have one spiritual heart. Love unites! Therefore, when you are consecrated to my Immaculate Heart, you are consecrated to my Son. As Mother, I bring you to Jesus. The Sacred and Immaculate Hearts have been sent to gather the family of man; to give back to the Eternal Father his creation which has wandered far from Him.

I have come to prepare you for times of great turmoil. These times are already upon us! Suffering is increasing due to sin, which is rampant. And in these days when God has granted Satan a time to test His people, you who are striving to love and serve God are being tempted continuously! Take courage, little ones! Remember that the devil's fury is limited and his time on earth is running out. He will not be permitted to roam the earth for much longer. Continue to resist him and all his evil ways!

Draw everything you need from God. Empty yourselves so that the Holy Spirit can fill you with His Presence and grace. Imitate my Son and His sacrifice of love. There are many saints of this age; many who are co-redeeming souls.

I come to prepare the way for my Son! First comes the purification of the world in which my Son's passion will be reflected. Many people have been chosen to prepare the way with me and the spirit of prophecy is blessing every nation toward the fulfillment of all that has been prophesied. You can become the saints of this age, giving birth to a new era, if you suffer everything unto God for love of Him. Trust in God! As you observe the world crumble around you, the world as you know it passes, your faith in Jesus will sustain you. Therefore, be at peace and pray for the conversion of sinners and nonbelievers. I will assist you to hold fast to the faith. Pray fervently. It is urgent! I love you. Your Mother

15. **10-10-96**
A Trial of Faith

Following Mass I prayed, "My Jesus, I love You and beg Your grace to sustain me in this trial. I am suffering so many temptations against faith. I observe very good souls who are seemingly close to You, suffering every type of loss and undergoing tests and temptations, which try them severely. Must your friends drink of such bitter suffering?"

Jesus said: *Soul of My cross, My closest friends are formed in the same manner as the Son of God and Son of Man. It is a great blessing to be chosen to co-redeem with Me. Good and holy souls are formed by means of tests of faith, hope, and love. And they are made strong through resistance to temptations. I permit this with confidence because I know that I supply these souls with every necessary grace and protection. My friends rejoice with Me when they see that their suffering, testing, temptations and trials have brought forth fruit, pure and holy, good and beautiful.

Such formation enriches the soul and the Mystical Body (Church). My closest friends are surrendered souls who desire only My Divine Will. They trust in My way and seek true wisdom. Having entered into union with Me, they are confident in the power of Divine Love and do not fear the tests of faith. They grow to carry the cross for the sake of pure love of Me.

*Soul of My cross, you faith is being tested as the weight of the cross bears down upon you and your loved ones. You are a victim of My Love, My lamb, upon the altar of sacrifice and I am forming you by means of this cross to trust in Me. My strong arm upholds you and My Divine Love sustains your poor little soul. My Divine Touch heals the lacerations of your heart.

Offer this test of faith, this trial and cross, to Me. Give everything as offering, as a sacrifice of praise to My Holy Name for love of Me. I will take your offering to My Heart and streams of grace will flow onto other souls because you chose to give Me your "fiat."

This Heart of Mine is lacerated also. It aches with pain as it bears the burden of mankind's guilt. This Heart of Mine is rejected and blasphemed. Won't you share a small portion of My Passion? Won't you offer reparation for the sin of the world? Today, My Mystical Body is being scourged from within and without and most of mankind is indifferent! But the cries of My just people do not fall on deaf ears. For I am not an indifferent God. I am the Good Shepherd who shall gather the flock together in My Sacred Heart. Though they have scattered all over the earth and wandered far from My voice; though My sheep are hungry and do not know where to find food that lasts; I will open My mouth and call them each by name to gather close to Me so that I can lead them to green pastures and streams of living water.

My lamb, as you are purified through the cross, so too, shall the earth be purified. As your household suffers and appears divided, so too, shall Mine. But this division will be temporary and will end in true restoration.

The good and holy things which have been taken for granted will be taken away for a period of time and this will create a hunger and thirst for what is sacred. For a short period of time, it will appear that My Eucharistic Sacrifice has vanished as an abomination is set upon the altar. The True Sacrifice of the Altar will remain with you, but in a hidden fashion. During this trial of faith, My Holy Spirit will be your Guide and His gifts will abide with you. And you shall be formed into My purest flock, a holy people, raised in sanctity unlike any previous generation.

*Soul of My cross, My lamb and victim for many, love Me as I love you. I am the Divine Bridegroom urging you to be still in My divine embrace though it is on the cross that all of this takes place. You shall not falter as you are safe in Me. You are persecuted for My sake and thus you draw grace, which saves many souls. Offer no resistance, My bride. Knowing that you are Mine, surrender and say with Me, "Father, not mine, but Your Will be done. Amen and I love you." *Soul, we are one heart. Peace. I love you. Your Jesus

16. **10-13-96** My home, AM
Obey Because You Love Me

Soul of My Cross, My bride and My altar,
You give Me honor and glory when you write all that I am doing in your soul. Write for Me. My Majesty is served when

you obey. My Sovereignty is over you, but I do not treat you as a slave. Do not obey Me out of duty. That is not much different from a slave whose freedom has been taken by his master. Will to obey Me from your heart because you love Me. Your Redeemer seeks your love. Let your obedience flow from love. I have revealed My Face to you. I have revealed that I love you and you know it. You are free because of that knowledge. Freedom has its responsibility. My work in your soul reaches beyond your personal sanctity. Through these writings, many will enjoy a new freedom - the freedom to Love! My Peace. Your Jesus

17. **10-17-96** Feast of St. Ignatius of Antioch. On Retreat.
The Blood of The Martyrs: Foundation of Church

Following the Chaplet of Divine Mercy with Father, Jesus said: **Please write for Me.**

On this day of remembrance of St. Ignatius (of Antioch), **I bless you and remind you of the blood of the martyrs which comingled with Mine to form the foundation of My Roman Catholic Church. The foundations set for you in My Mystical Body are indestructible. My Holy Spirit empowered the early Church and they were zealous for souls and full of Love, which enables one to lay down his life for another.**

Let it be known, beloved creation, that your age also requires martyrs. And that My Spirit will empower many to sacrifice for My Mystical Body which is wounded and bleeding. My Blood will be joined with the blood of more martyrs of this age to purify My Church and the world.

My Foundations are indestructible! My Traditions are holy and full of Life! My Life is for you! New Life is yours through sacrifice because reparation is due. Wayward people, I will search you out and bring you back to Me.

My Church will be glorious and she will be your refuge and fountain of Grace. Blessed are you who believe! Hold fast to your Faith, the Truth and My Word! I am your Stronghold, your firm Foundation, and in Me, you will be able to endure as

the early Church endured persecution for the faith. And you will assist Me to raise up a Glorified Body.

Many generations will look back at this age and praise Me. And the Father will be glorified, because through you, sacrificial lambs, victims of love, My Body will be healed and made radiantly beautiful for all the world.

The Community of Saints intercedes with you. Come! The Good Shepherd calls you to Himself. You know My Voice. Follow Me. Build upon the foundations set before you long ago. These foundations are filled with the blood of the martyrs who paid the cost of discipleship.

Be courageous and invoke the Holy Spirit always. The Spirit, with His Bride, lead the battle against the evil of this age. For love of Me, become a soldier in the army formed through the intercession of the Immaculate Heart.

My Spirit will sanctify you. Do not be afraid! Love is your weapon and its power overcomes everything. For only a short time, it will appear that My Church is in ruins. Then, from her deepest foundations, shall arise her Majestic Glory!

I am calling you to become a part of the foundation! Do you love Me enough to answer the call? I await your fiat because My Hands are tied until you give your yes to My request.

Let Me hear you say, "Yes, Lord, I will die for Love of you! I will fight for Your Holy Name! I will do whatever You tell me to do because I love You and want only to serve You and live eternally in Your Kingdom! I want to do the Father's Will to give Him glory by my small sacrifice. Allow Me to be part of the Love that is to restore the world!"

And I will respond, "Come, follow Me. I will lead you to green pastures and streams of living water! I will satisfy your thirst with My Love. You will be My people and I will be your God. And the darkness will be no more! O How I long for it because I want to be One with you forever."

But there is much work to do first! Evil must be trampled underfoot and the sheep and the goats must be separated. Pray and be at peace. I love you. Your Jesus

18. **10-22-96** Rosary with my Spiritual Director, my home.
The Heart of Our Redeemer

Father led the Sorrowful Mysteries of the Rosary and prayed that Mary would take us into the Sacred Heart of Jesus. Immediately, Mary seemingly took us there. There were many chambers, full of riches. I noticed the profound silence of His Heart.

Our Lady said: *My dear children, I am with you to lead you into the very Heart of Our Redeemer. Come. Do not delay. His Heart will heal your heart. His Heart is the remedy for the world. Pray with me. Open your heart to me so that I may lead you quickly into the refuge of His Sacred Heart. Live in the sanctuary of His Holy Heart. Within, you will be made holy. You cannot know love if you do not know His Heart. Allow me to guide you there by the power of the Holy Spirit. Pray and you will gain knowledge and understanding. The light of love is for you. All good things await you.*

Awaken, my dear children, grace awaits your invitation. Desire it and it shall be yours. He stands at the door and knocks. Awaken from your slumber that you may no longer sleep in darkness. Evil is the thief of love and peace. The disorder of the world will be displaced by the ordered love of God. Why do you settle for so little, my children? Scarcely do you recognize evil from good. Humble yourselves. Ask for the light of the Holy Spirit. Seek His Wisdom, not the worlds. The enemy strikes in your mind. If you do not seek the mind of God, by the power of the Holy Spirit, you will be led by falsehood and error. Sin will hold you in bondage. Look inside to your own heart. See the emptiness. Acknowledge your own insecurities and fears. Seek the security of the Sacred Heart of our Redeemer. His Love will cast out your fear. You suffer because there is so little faith in the world. Ask the Holy Spirit to increase your faith. Pray for this. Come to the fountain of grace that builds up faith, hope and love, contained in the Eucharistic Jesus, available to you every day at every Mass. Eat of His Flesh and drink of His Blood, and you will be transfigured by grace. He will live in you. You have all that is necessary, but you do not partake. My Heart is grieved by this. Is it any wonder that your suffering increases? Pray that you may know the Heart of Our Redeemer. His True Presence is with you always.

The sin of the world and the darkness of this age cannot change His everlasting covenant of love. He is over everything. The devil roams freely for a short while only. He claims many souls in the darkness of this age. If you decide for God, He will assist you with all necessary grace. If you are indecisive, you will falter and be lost. The prayers, sacrifices, sufferings of fervent souls, alive with love, are needed to avert the loss of souls who have not yet decided for God. Pray fervently for the conversion of the world and for the salvation of all souls. Invoke the Holy Spirit and St. Michael, the warrior and protector of souls. Hide in my maternal heart, and I will take you to the Sacred and Holy Heart of Jesus, the Savior of the world. Do not delay. I love you. Your Mother

19. **10-22-96 (B)** Continued
Priests Crowned with a Crown of Thorns

At the Third Sorrowful Mystery, the Crowning of Thorns, I saw Jesus, crowned with thorns, blood flowing down His Holy Face, led out to the crowd. He stood before them, silent and still in His suffering. They jeered and spat on Him. He was ridiculed and mocked. He offered no defense. The hatred of the crowd and the evil of the situation was intense. Suddenly, He was transfigured into a modern day priest. Then one priest after another took His place. Each was crowned with thorns, mocked and ridiculed.

Jesus spoke: **My beloved shepherds, fear not. I am with you. You are My image and likeness, My Body, My Presence in the world. My faithful priests, you will be ridiculed for holding fast to My holy traditions. You will be mocked for loving and proclaiming the truth. You will be scorned by modern day philosophers. Progressive "thinkers" will impose themselves upon you and My faithful flock. There will be times of suffering and difficulty for you. There will be a period of time when the authority of Peter** (Rome) **and the authority of the Roman Catholic Church will be undermined. Confusion has already begun. My Body is already divided. The sheep will follow the True Shepherd. The goats will scatter to their own agendas and philosophies.**

Recall that My apparent defeat resulted in victory that is eternal. My victory is yours, My good and faithful servants. My Word stands, a lamp unto your feet. Hold fast to your faith, hope and charity. You are witnessing a crisis of faith already. The Holy Spirit will equip you with every necessary gift and grace. My covenant with you stands eternally. Blessed are you, My brother priests, chosen for this time in history; you will witness My Goodness, My Mercy, My Light overshadows all of creation to transfigure it into My Holiness. I shall equip you. You will bear witness to Me even as the crown of thorns bears down on your head, causing you to suffer very much. Your sacrifice unites you to Me. Ours is an embrace of love. Your hands are consecrated instruments, empowered by the Holy Spirit to change bread and water into My Body and Blood. Continue to feed My flock the Bread of Life. Do not compromise this Sacrament in any way! Feed My sheep the necessary nourishment of life. Do not let them starve when I have consecrated your hands to feed them. Lead My sheep by example of your own faith and hope. Bring them to Me by the way of love. Your own heart must not be a desert land. Pray always that I may fill you. Do not be afraid, because Divine Providence is over you. I will be your strength; the Holy Spirit will light your way; the Blessed Mother will be your refuge. Consecrate your heart to hers, so that her heart can permeate yours with holy virtues.

I have raised up an army of lay faithful, empowering them with many gifts, that My Body may be enriched and fortified for these trying times. The Holy Spirit will guide you to find one another. I have never been concerned with "numbers." That is a human way of thinking. With Me, a few affect the many. A few, truly holy priests go a long way toward the salvation of many souls. Humility attracts Me. To the humble, I give very much. Ask for all the gifts of the Holy Spirit and believe they are yours. Your priesthood is a continual martyrdom, if you are faithful to My way and My law of love.

I have gone before you that I may be your consolation and hope. I have prepared a place for you in My Father's House. You are crowned with suffering but for a moment compared to the eternity of glory that is yours. Strive to be holy for Me.

Pray always so that you do not falter or lead My sheep astray. Pray for one another. Pray especially for priests in authority who persecute you. Never judge one another, but always pray fervently that all will be brought back to Me by way of the truth. The devils that are free to roam the earth now target you in ever increasing attacks on all sides. Be aware. Know the enemy and his tactics that you may battle effectively. Strive to keep your peace in the midst of the turmoil that surrounds you. This is possible only if you pray very much. Frequent the Sacraments of Holy Communion and Reconciliation. Provide these for My faithful always. Come to Me for everything. I will always be with you. You are Mine. I love you unconditionally, My beloved shepherds. I give you My own courage. Peace I give to you. Your Jesus

20. **10-23-96** Rosary with my Spiritual Director, my home (Glorious Mysteries).

Follow the Vicar of Christ and Return to the Eucharist

Our Lady said: *My dear little children, follow the Vicar of Christ, Pope John Paul II, in his preparation for the year 2000. There are many graces available through his plan for the Church and the world. As this year comes to a close, as winter approaches, prepare for the year dedicated to Christ Jesus* (1997). *Return to the Eucharist! Adore the Blessed Sacrament. Come, pray before the Tabernacle from your heart. The Eucharistic Heart of Jesus will heal you, my dear children. Make every effort to receive the Eucharistic Jesus as often as possible. Often as you eat His Flesh and drink His Blood, you will be healed and blessed. There will be many reconciliations, healings and supernatural graces available as more of you return to the Eucharist. Incomprehensible grace is yours through the Eucharist. Your hearts should be filled with gratitude for this Holy Sacrament, which gains for the world the Father's Divine Mercy. The Holy Sacrifice of the Mass is the fountain of the Father's Mercy upon the world, because it is the Body, Blood, Soul and Divinity of His Son. My Son remains with you through this Sacrament. Do not take it for granted.*

My children, you have wandered far from God. Come back by means of the Eucharist so that you can be healed of all that is unholy. As souls return to the Eucharist, there will be the healing of individual souls, families, cities, and nations. Jesus will transfigure more souls into Himself to perpetuate His Presence on earth. More souls will be raised to intercession for the world. These souls will come against the evil in these trying days, when evil is rampant, blatantly roaming the earth to devour unsuspecting souls, families, cities, nations.

In the year about to begin, there will be more division between that which is good and that which is evil. Both will increase. Good will increase in goodness and holiness, becoming stronger and able to suffer for the sake of love. Evil will become darker, more hideous, in blatant attacks on souls, especially families, youth, priests, and women. When you observe your loved ones touched by evil influences, falling into temptations, pray fervently, with faith and hope. Continue to love them. Love is the law of God. Offer sacrifice for them. (e.g., fasting). Trust. Through your intercession, in God's time, they will be converted. Light will come. Offer all of your suffering to God in intercession for His Divine Plan for the world.

My dear children, you must draw from the Eucharistic Jesus, so that you can love and be at peace in the midst of turmoil. You must pray very much in adoration of the Blessed Sacrament, so that you can persevere through these difficult times. I will assist you to have faith for those who are losing faith, have hope for those who are losing hope, have love for those who do not have love. As you intercede, I will multiply grace through My Immaculate Heart, so that every soul who desires conversion shall have it. Praise the Father, Eternal Light, for the gift of His Only Son in the Eucharist.

Praise Jesus for redeeming the world with His Precious Blood. Praise the Holy Spirit who is with you as Counselor, bearing witness to the truth. He gives you wisdom, knowledge, understanding of the truth. You are the lambs who follow one voice, the voice of the Good Shepherd. Your shepherd on earth is the Vicar of Christ Jesus. He leads according to the authority given to him by the Most Holy Trinity. I am with him to guide you. Be at peace. I love you, my dear little children. Your Mother

21. **10-24-96** My home, 7:30 AM.
I Thirst

I prayed, "Jesus, I thirst for love!" Jesus said, **My bride and My victim, I am with you. You are on the cross with Me. I give you My own thirst for Love. Console Me, Soul.**

Jesus, how can I console You, My Lord? I am dying of thirst, already adhered to the cross for love of You. Will You give me to drink of Your Love?

Soul of My cross, hang on the wood with Me. See what I see. You are drinking My Love, but the more that you drink the greater your thirst. We are one. Because I love, I thirst. Love loves. Soul, drink! My blood and water are a fountain for you. You have not yet understood; your thirst is My own thirst. Console Me.

Jesus, how?

Bring souls to Me! I thirst! Soul of My cross, our union is consummated on the cross. Together we cry out, "Abba"! "Abba, I am the ransom, the victim lamb; cancel the debt, gather the flock, lead them home." Soul, the pain you feel is My own. From the cross, we cry out, "God is Love. Come." Few hear our cry. Fewer come. Soul of My cross, you are My consolation. My Divine Will is reigning in you. Because you are silent and hidden, My Majesty abounds in you. I have lifted the veil. Your silent suffering has rendered you pure in My sight. Your obedience consoles Me in this age of disobedience. The cross has transfigured you. Will you gather souls to alleviate My thirst?

How, Lord?

Do whatever I tell you; go wherever I send you. Suffer silently. Permit Me to use you whenever I ask; wait prayerfully, patiently, for My command. Do everything with Me, and realize always, we are together as one heart of love. Love alone draws souls. Holiness draws souls. Mercy and humility draws souls. Do you understand now, your thirst is My own? First, I caused you to thirst for Me. Now, I cause you to thirst for souls, because you are with Me and in Me. You love with My own limitless Love, because you exist inside My Heart of Infinite Love. My thirst continues.

Lord, will You always thirst?

Soul, I will thirst until the last soul is gathered home. My thirst will be quenched when I stand before the Father and say, "Father, I have brought them all to You. I did not lose one of those You gave to Me." Until then, I thirst! My thirst is your thirst now. My intention is your intention. Yes, My bride?

Yes, My Jesus.

Do you love Me, Soul?

Entirely, Jesus. Do you love me, Lord?

Entirely, soul, entirely. Offer Me everything. Your suffering is a fragrant perfume, rising to the heavens and drawing grace upon many souls. Like all the brides who have gone before you, proclaiming the Gospel with their very lives, you are radiantly beautiful in My sight. You hoped to be an eagle for Me, but I desired to make you a dove first. Bless Me, My bride. Thank Me for what I have done for you.

Jesus, My Lord, My Savior, I bless Your Holy Name eternally. Gratitude fills my heart. Thank you for all that You have done for my poor soul. Your Sacred Heart is my fascination, my unending desire. Your Almighty hand has created me anew. I offered my life to You and You took it. You lavished me with Love. Every heavenly grace became mine. You are ever faithful to me, My Jesus. You never change, yesterday, today and always. You raise me up and up, giving me every good thing. You raised me to the cross with You, that, I too, might hang between heaven and earth, to intercede for the salvation of the world. You put fire within me that I might co-redeem souls. That fire is love which co-redeems. O my Jesus, it seems there is nothing You would not do for me. You provide everything. You reign in me, Lord. You have conquered. I have Your heart; now I have charity. I have Your mind; now I have wisdom, knowledge and understanding. I have Your eyes; now I have vision. Jesus, I have everything in You. I thirst as You thirst and suffer as You suffer. Together my Lord, let us gather souls for the Father. O Lamb of God, make me Your altar of sacrifice. There is much work to be done toward the salvation of souls. Let us work together, one forever, in love. Bless me, Lord, with Your love again and again. Thank You for bending to me.

Soul of My cross, you have consoled the Lord, your God. Bear fruit for Me, My bride, bear fruit. Lean on Me in your

suffering. Rest in Me always. You are covered in My Love. Your Groom reigns in you. I am pleased. I love you. Raise your voice to the Father. Draw grace for the world. I am your Jesus.

22. **10-31-96**
Reminder of His Sacrifice

It is Halloween, which in many ways has become the devil's holiday. Father and I prayed the Rosary. After a while, I felt heat in the palms of my hands, and pressure and as if a very sharp object was driven into the palms, tearing the flesh. Each thrust pierced deeper and became more painful. I asked Father to bind and cast out any evil spirit, which would mock the piercing of Jesus' Hands or any vain imagination. Father prayed over me and discerned that this was a grace from God and part of the prayer of union. Father said, "Offer it up to God." I did as he asked. On Halloween, it seemed fitting that I be reminded of His sacrifice and enter into reparation for sin.

23. **11-1-96** Feast of All Saints
Image of Hope

In the morning, during Holy Hour following Mass, prayer was difficult. Yet I remained before the Tabernacle in a pitiful state knowing that Jesus would gaze upon my soul's misery and grant mercy!

Later at home, I suddenly received an interior image of God, the Father, high up in the heavens and the earth far below. Suddenly, the Father breathed a powerful wind, which passed from heaven to earth and covered it. Light, magnificent light, filled every corner of the earth and the darkness was no more. Heavenly, Divine Light overcame creation. The Father's breath is Love. The wind is the Holy Spirit. The Light is Jesus.

24. **11-2-96**
Pure Grace

My heart is pierced almost constantly throughout the day and I prayed unceasingly in the spirit as I went about my duties around the house. Peace, strength and joy filled my soul. Even in the midst of a difficult family situation, I never lost my peace of soul and offered everything up to God joyfully. Pure grace!

25. **11-3-96**
Sorrow for the Youth

I was restless throughout the night and felt the pain in my hands again. I had the strongest sense of Jesus on the cross and His sorrow for today's "youth."

Jesus said: **I am merciful and compassionate toward the youth of this age. They are victims of a lack of love; a lack of teaching. My Divine Love will rescue you, My little ones! My Light will draw you out of the darkness. I, Myself, will become your Teacher! I will reach out for you and bring you back to My Heart so you will know Love! The enemy targets you to bring you to ruin. But I will raise you up to be holy. I am with you always. I love you. I am your Jesus.**

26. **11-4-96**
America Re-crucifying Jesus

At morning Mass when the priest raised the Host and said, "This is the Lamb of God, who takes away the sins of the world," it felt like a scalpel had been thrust into my heart tissue. In a situation, which tempts me to close my heart, Divine Grace comes to cause me to remain open to love. Following Mass, while praying before the Tabernacle, I went into contemplation. Then, I saw the following:

1) I saw the map of the United States. An American flag was laid over the land. Then, a wooden cross that spanned from north

to south and east to west was placed on top of the flag. Jesus took His place on the wooden cross. Nails were hammered into His hands and feet. Then a sword pierced His side. Blood and water gushed onto the American flag, penetrating the soil. Jesus' disposition was utterly sorrowful for our country.

2) The scene changed to a farmland image. It was the season of the harvesting of the wheat. The farm hands were carrying sheaves of wheat. Jesus said: **Soul, look closely.** I saw that the ends of the sheaves of wheat were stained with blood. Jesus continued: **Soul, the blood of the innocents covers the country (USA). Innocent blood marks and stains everything this country produces, even the good. The aborted babies are a blood sacrifice to Satan. That blood sacrifice acts as a magnet to draw more evil upon the land. This country, the land of plentitude, carries out My crucifixion again!**

3) Again, I saw Jesus on the cross that spanned the flag and the country. Now, Jesus put me on the cross with Him. My heart is pierced also.

4) Then, I saw a multitude of dark spirits, lifting up a platform upon which sat the President and his wife (Clinton's). The dark spirits were hailing them as King and Queen. They raised the platform up high for the entire world to see and all eyes were upon them.

5) The image changed. I saw the entire country covered with huge tractors which were rototilling the soil, every inch of it. Jesus said: **At the end of one season and beginning of another season, the soil must be completely turned over. I, Myself, will uproot and replant! I, the Lord, your God, will do it! Pray, dear soul, for your country. Suffer with Me! America, I gave you so much! The favor of the Most Holy Trinity was yours! What have you done with it? You are turning from Me. You are turning from life to death. Repent or your pride will lead to your fall. Turn back to Me so that I can lead you out of your present darkness! My watchful Eye is over you, America! Decide for life! I am your Jesus!**

6) It is the eve of the election (11-4-96) and Jesus repeated these words: **Tomorrow, you turn a new page.** Jesus' disposition was very sorrowful and grave!

27. 11-7-96
The Need to Accept God's Forgiveness

Prayer: "My Jesus, You are the Divine Teacher! You lead my soul by darkness while flooding me with light for other souls. You are curing me of selfishness and I sense charity and zeal growing in my soul. Jesus, I am your pupil and I love Your teaching. Cause me to be who You want me to be through service to other souls. Amen."

In the evening, a priest prayed over me and then asked that I pray over him. As I did so, grace came to me and I received the words, "Spirit of guilt." I told the priest and he offered up a prayer to God the Father about his past sins.

Immediately following this, I heard God the Father say: **The Blood of the Lamb has washed you clean, inside and outside.** I received an image of the priest covered in the Precious Blood. The Eternal Father repeated His words with great majesty, power and authority. Then He said: **My Son, you are forgiven. But you have not ACCEPTED My forgiveness!**

Say to Me, "Father, I accept Your forgiveness. Jesus, I accept Your forgiveness. Holy Spirit, I accept Your forgiveness."

Jesus said: **Mercy is Mine to give and yours to accept.**

Then the Holy Spirit said: **Reject the spirit of guilt for sins which have been confessed. When the spirit of guilt attacks you, resist! Do not accept the lies. Ask for the Spirit of Truth always. This night, you are given an angel to assist you.**

Then I heard a voice, which was different from the Father, Son, or Holy Spirit, yet it had power of presence and authority. I heard, "My name is the Light of Truth." This is to be this priest's special angel to help him in the spiritual battle.

Then I received an image of this priest's soul represented by neatly raked soil. Everything appeared well yet in the deeper layers was buried a big root ball. As this priest ACCEPTED God's forgiveness, this was uprooted from the depths of the soil. Repressed guilt could not take root in the soul anymore. It was evident that this priest received a new freedom through acceptance of God's forgiveness.

28. **11-9-96**
Tears of Blood for the Church

While praying next to my spiritual director in the apparition room of a conference where Our Lady would appear to Ivan D., I was bombarded with temptations and overcome with negativity about spiritual realities. I prayed to St. Michael, the Archangel and immediately, the temptations ended and I entered prayer. Instantly, I saw the most beautiful face of Jesus as in the Shroud Image. My gaze fixed on the countenance of His Majestic Face. He said: **Soul, put your hands up to My Face, please.**

I did as He asked, positioning my hands below His chin, as if to cradle His Face in my hands (so to speak). I gazed intently into His Eyes and saw them as pools of Pure Love. Suddenly, a tear of Blood flowed from each eye, down His cheek and into the palms of my hands. Suddenly the image included St. John Lateran's Basilica in Rome. I observed the blood tears flow upon the Church (represented by the Basilica). Overcome by His sorrow, I asked, "Lord what are you teaching me?" The Holy Spirit reminded me that St. John Lateran is the seat of the Bishop of Rome, Pope John Paul II. Then I asked, "Lord, do you weep for Your Church?"

He said: **Yes, I weep for My Church. My Mystical Body is deeply afflicted. She is racked by pride, division, and disobedience infiltrating the Magesterium, spreading confusion to the faithful causing apostasy and despair among the members.**

But My Holy Spirit flows like an endless fountain through My Vicar for this age, John Paul. The world is blessed by Me through My Vicar. Hold fast to the teachings he has deposited in the Church. Hold fast to My Holy Traditions, the Truth, set forth in the foundation that I, Myself, have set for you. The deposit of faith protected by My Vicar is the world's treasury of salvation.

I came among you, My creation, to overcome the prince of the world who is your enemy. I instituted the Church to be My Living Presence, My Body on earth, so that you also will overcome the prince of the world. My Body (Church) is the vehicle of Divine Grace for the world. My people, you fail to see the gift that you have in her. The enemy himself knows it and aims to dismember her. You are confused about who your enemy is

in the world. You question the Church's authority. Her authority comes from Me, your Lord and Savior. But her authority is being undermined by the enemy so that you are confused about the truth and what is good and what is evil. There is enough smoke in the sanctuary to confuse a multitude of souls!

Fear not! I will restore My Mystical Body! She will be restored to a holy House of Prayer. She is your Mother! The dragon that blows the smoke into My Sanctuary will be slain by the Woman Clothed with the Sun who wears twelve stars for her crown. His time draws to a close rapidly.

Dear soul, I am sorrowful for all the souls who are deeply affected by the confusion and division in the Church. Many are led away along the path of perdition. When a soul loses the gift of faith, it has lost the most precious gift! Without faith, souls are blind. The loss of souls is the cause of My tears of blood. Weep with Me and offer yourself as a sacrifice to save souls with Me. Together, our sacrifice flows onto the Church transforming her. The enemy is defeated by the Blood of the Lamb.

The smoke that the enemy has blown into My Sanctuary will be blown out by the Wind of the Holy Spirit. By the power of love, it will be purified and restored. Be My little lamb, sacrifice and work with Me. I love you and give you My Peace through faith. I am your Jesus.

Shortly, Ivan arrived and led the group of fifty in seven "Our Father's", seven "Hail Mary's", and seven "Glory Be's." Then Our Lady appeared to him. I kept my eyes closed and remained in a deep state of prayer. Peace came and all skepticism left me.

I said, "Mary, my Mother, I love you with all of my heart. My family needs your help! Please!" Interiorly, I heard her voice. *I am helping your family. And I am helping all families. Have hope! St. Joseph is watching over your family also. Pray and sacrifice. Offer everything to God.*

29. **11-10-96**
Do Not Worry

During a Marian convention Mass, after Holy Communion, I heard Our Lady interiorly.

My child, be at peace. Do not worry. Offer your suffering up to God. It is a pleasing offering in His Eyes and you draw grace for many. My daughter, God is with you! Your family is blessed through your sacrifice. You have placed God before all and, therefore, you are richly graced by Him.

There are many graces in store for you and your family. Daughter, in Nazareth there were many days and nights of silence and solitude. The mysteries of God are wonders to be pondered. Prayer and reflection in silence is time well spent. Through prayer, light is given to a soul to enrich and purify.

Be faithful to writing of the graces in your soul, my daughter. It will bear fruit for many souls. Rest in my heart little one. I will console you. You are not alone. You are rich with heavenly friendship. I love you. I am your Mother

30. **11-10-96 (B)**
Come Together to Worship and Be Blessed

Following a Marian convention, at home I asked Our Lady, "Are you pleased by conferences such as this?" I heard: M*y child, often as people come together to pray and worship my Son, I am pleased. And in assemblies such as these, my presence is permitted in order to distribute the many heavenly graces which flow through my Immaculate Heart.*

Souls need encouragement along the way of holiness. Assemblies such as this offer encouragement to many. The way of holiness is not easy. You cannot walk it alone. Gathering together to pray, to teach, to bear witness to God's Presence and Grace is uplifting for all! When you strive to live the messages of Medjugorje, you strive to be holy. I come from heaven to aid you in your journey.

I am joyful to observe so many priests gathered together. To my sons, my beloved priests, become beacons of holiness because holiness attracts souls to God and that is the purpose of your priestly ministry.

Blessed are you, beloved children, who believe without seeing! My apparitions bear witness to God's love for you. You are called to holiness because God is holy and you are created for union with Him. Holiness is yours by Divine Grace. You must pray very much to know and understand the workings of God's grace in your soul and in the world. Holiness is a gift that is within your reach. God's love and mercy make it so.

Thank you for responding to my call. Strive to live my messages for the sake of love and peace in the world. Your efforts affect many souls as you draw grace for the salvation of the world. I love and bless you in the name of the Most Holy Trinity. I am your Mother.

31. 11-11-96
For a Priest Dying of Cancer

"My beloved brother and priest, Father Luke, you have enriched My Mystical Body with love. Your life of sacrifice gives glory to the Eternal Father. You have served Me, your Lord and Savior, faithfully. Your good works have blessed countless souls. You are a pure vessel of My Holy Spirit. You glorify My Holy Name by fulfilling your vocation as priest and minister to My people. Your vocation to intercession is never ending. Your consecrated hands shall continue to work for Me until every soul is gathered in My Father's House. Do not be afraid. My grace shall lead you gently, peacefully. Resist temptation. Your faith is not in vain. You are Mine and I shall never abandon you. Rest in My Sacred Heart of Love. Allow My Mother and yours, to anoint you with the oil of Divine Love. Trust. My Holy Spirit is in you. I love you and thank you My faithful priest. The angels and saints are your family. You are never alone. Receive My Peace. Your Jesus." My Spiritual Director read this to Father Luke. They were blessed powerfully!

32. 11-12-96
St. Francis about Union and St. Clare about The Eucharist

Out of town in a Mission Church, I prayed by the statue of St. Francis of Assisi. The first manuscript of writings had just been delivered to the publisher.

"Dear St. Francis, thank you for your assistance in this mission and intercession for my soul." I heard St. Francis say, "Little, little one, leave everything into the hands of Almighty God. (Refers to the mission of these writings.) For yourself, unite yourself on the cross to our Beloved Lord and Savior. Suffer in union with Him. He will pierce your heart with Divine Love and cause living waters to flow from your soul so that others drink of your union of love. He will wound you so that your blood co-mingles as a sacrifice that is salvific for souls. He will crown you with thorns to mark you as "Bride of Christ." Love the cross, little dove. Rest peacefully upon your Savior. He will do the rest. I bless you in His Holy Name. Be pure for your Divine Bridegroom. Give honor, praise and thanksgiving to the Lord forever."

After a brief silence St. Francis said, "Behold! St. Clare."

Then I heard St. Clare say, "The Eucharist will be held up before many opposing armies to overcome the evil of this age."

(I understood that many movements within the Church would become Eucharistic movements, emphasizing this Sacrament to overcome those which aim to diminish the Eucharist in the world.) Then came an image of St. Clare holding up the Monstrance with the Blessed Sacrament and her figure was practically lost in the brilliance of the Blessed Sacrament. She held the Monstrance before an attacking army, which quickly retreated. St. Clare appeared to be in ecstasy in adoration of the Blessed Sacrament. She had the utmost confidence in the power of the Eucharist.

The image ended and St. Clare continued. "Eat of the Bread of Life as often as possible. Jesus' Body, Blood, Soul, and Divinity will be the sustenance that sustains the remnant Church in its hour of great trial and persecution. Even if the true Sacrament is driven into the hidden corners of the world, its power cannot be diminished. There is nothing to fear. Have confidence in God. Serve Him humbly. I bless you." She whispered her name "Clare" and was gone.

33. **11-14-96** After 8:30 AM Mass
A Message from St. Joseph to Families

During Holy Hour, I prayed for families and marriages because so many are being torn apart. I wondered why heaven didn't protect families from all the evil that targets them in this age. Suddenly, I heard St. Joseph speak.

First, it seems to me, that in the Communion of Saints there is a varying degree of perfection in heaven. It seems that St. Joseph has a most unique and high state of perfection. When St. Joseph speaks to my soul, he speaks with a felt wisdom, gentleness and patience. His presence is not overpowering but gentle, extremely kind, filled with charity. His authority seems to come from holiness of the highest state before God. It seems very clear to my soul that Jesus and Mary listen to St. Joseph's pleas. Among the Communion of Saints it seems he is of the highest rank. Clearly, I understood that the Church, families (especially fathers of families) are under his patronage. He said: (very slowly and tenderly)

"My dear little child,

When the Lord Jesus walked on the earth, many of us awaited the manifestation of His Kingdom and Glory. Often Jesus said, "First, the Son of Man must be rejected, suffer much and die." The Glory of God came after the fulfillment of these words. The words of Scripture came to pass. There are prophecies for this age, which must be fulfilled. There is suffering which must come upon the earth to purge the evil of this age. Suffering is and always has been a part of man's journey. Suffering is redemptive when united to Jesus. The trials of purification turn man's heart toward God and away from himself.

Dear child, do not be discouraged when you see suffering. Rather let it be a catalyst for more prayer and sacrifice. Trust in Divine Providence, for God is perfect in Wisdom, Goodness, and Grace. God will restore the family of man, but first there are trials, tribulations, and purifications, which must come to pass. I intercede with the Blessed Virgin Mary for every family. Satan knows that his time is short so he bombards families and marriages with every evil tactic. But he will not be victorious. Remember child, what appears to be divided can be reunited. Many are being tried and purified because Jesus and Mary must be the center of every heart, every marriage, and every family. Prayer is the glue that holds families together. Even one family member dedicated to prayer and sacrifice for the sake of all other members, can gain for them, the grace of conversion. Families must be patient with one another, always living the law of love for each member. Pray especially for those whose faith is dormant or very, very small.

Dear child, you cannot fathom what God has prepared for those who faithfully follow Him. Heaven is beyond any human comprehension; too sublime for words. Whatever suffering there is on earth, it pales compared to the reward in heaven. Therefore, grow in patience in the midst of suffering. It is pleasing to God that you have compassion for families and marriages. This is a grace given to you so that you would intercede for all families. Jesus will manifest His Glory for the entire world to see. He will restore the earth at the precise time ordained by the Father. Do not be anxious, rather be at peace in the security of God's Love for each soul; for His entire creation.

I love you, little one. I intercede for your family at every moment. Be at peace. I pray your faith will be increased. (St.) Joseph, His worker."

34. **11-15-96**
Underground?

I saw vividly, the descent of the dove of the Holy Spirit into the center of the prayer group. It appeared that the floor opened up by His power and I saw a gaping hole in the floor into which the Holy Spirit descended. He filled the underground area with His Light. It became very beautiful because of His Presence. It reminded me of the catacombs in Rome to a certain extent.

I sensed there would be persecution to the Roman Catholic faithful. This persecution, however, will lead to new life in the Holy Spirit.

Prayer:

"O Holy Spirit of God,
where You lead, I will follow.
Abide in God's people.
Lead creation into Your Light.
Grant us True Life in You.
You are the Heart of the Church.

Breathe Your Life, Light, Love
into her members.
And through them
draw all the world to God.
O Holy Spirit,
where You are, there is no fear.
Live in us and make us Holy
for You are Holy! Holy! Holy!
Restore the earth
by the fire of Your Love.
O Holy Spirit of God,
Lead us always and everywhere.
Amen."

35. **11-19-96** My home, Rosary with my Spiritual Director.
Pope John Paul II in the Garden of Gethsemane

Father led the Sorrowful Mysteries. At the Agony in the Garden of Gethsemane, I saw Jesus bent over the rock, sweating blood. Oh! The darkness of that night of incomprehensible suffering culminating in the words, "Father, Not Mine But Your Will Be Done"!

Suddenly, the image of Jesus in agony changed to the image of Pope John Paul II in agony. It was as if I was in the garden with the Holy Father to observe him. I am studying the Holy Father closely and I observe him praying and so sorrowful. His sorrow is not for himself but for the faithful, the Church, the world, all of God's creation. He knows suffering will touch them all in a time of great confusion and tribulation, a time of a crisis of faith in the world. Then, I saw apostles lead the Pope out of the garden and into hiding so that those who wished to apprehend him, do not find him. Suddenly, there was silence in the garden.

Jesus says, **Beloved soul, write please.**

When Pope John Paul II is silenced, there will be a true crisis of faith and confusion will be widespread. In My mercy, this will be for a short time only. He will be protected by the faithful remnant, but his agony will be one of complete union with My agony. Even from a hidden place, his intercession

will affect the entire world. He is an offering for all in My image.

An impostor will bring dishonor to the Chair of Peter. Many souls will be misled. I will be merciful to the innocent souls. I will bring My Just Hand down upon the impostor and his cohorts. My true Church will be under the patronage of Pope John Paul, even as he is hidden because his presence and leadership will be made evident to the faithful remnant by the power of the Holy Spirit. To My Church, I say, hold fast to the truth and I am the Truth! In your hour of great need I, Myself, will guide you. Do not be afraid. My Covenant stands. My Church is glorious and victorious over all evil. Let Satan make his last stand. He will fall in defeat, crushed by the heel of the Blessed Virgin Mary, the Woman clothed with the Sun and wearing a crown of twelve stars. Our United Hearts will triumph! Fortify one another in faith, hope, and love. I, the Lord, your God, am with you. Do not be afraid! I love you. Your Jesus

I sensed great suffering for people at the loss of faith, at a time, when the very fabric of the Roman Catholic Church will be rent in various ways. The stability of all people will be affected and shaken. Yet, Jesus repeats twice in the message, **Do not be afraid. I am with you!!**

At the Scourging decade:

I saw a beautiful Monstrance on the altar with the Blessed Sacrament exposed and radiating brilliant light. The Blessed Sacrament changed into the image of Jesus at the time of His scourging in Jerusalem. I understood that the True Presence will be doubted, mocked, and subverted.

At the Crown of Thorns decade:

I saw a crown of thorns placed around a prayer cenacle. Jesus said: **This represents the ridicule and persecution that will befall the faithful who pray and hold fast to the faith. You will taste of My Passion so that our union will be complete.**

36. **11-20-96** My home, Rosary with Spiritual Director, Glorious Mysteries.

Padre Pio Speaks to His Brother Priest

At the end of the Rosary, Father went through the Litany of Saints. When he said Padre Pio's name, I heard these words. (Padre Pio's disposition was very serious, but most loving.)

"O my brother priest."
"Rejoice and give thanks to God for the divine grace in your soul.
Drink, my brother priest.
Drink of the divine grace that comes to you through the mercy of God.
Be fortified! Grow!
Allow the Holy Spirit to permeate your entirety.
Live in the Holy Spirit.
Breathe the Spirit in and breathe the Spirit out.
The time is coming and soon, I tell you,
that you will draw from every reserve within you.
You will be swimming against the current, my dear brother.
The Church has had her troubles in times past but this age is different.
Now is the time for that wretch, the beast who devours souls, to be chained in the abyss of death.
The Church will be thoroughly purified.
You will be amazed at the apostasy, division, scandal, and widespread loss of faith.
You will uphold many and aid souls to keep the faith.
My brother priest, I bless you
with my hand that bleeds still
for the love of Christ and for His Bride who suffers.
I am close to you.
We will fight the good fight together.
I will assist you to have strength to battle Satan
and his army as his attacks continue.
Be at peace. Do not worry. God is with you.
So too, am I.
Your brother priest, Pio"

At the part about swimming against the current, I had a vision of Father swimming upstream in a river with a very strong current. There were many souls traveling with the current. It took all of Father's strength and courage to swim against the current. There were souls following Father upstream. He paved the way for them.

37. **11-22-96** Friday AM, my home.
St. Joseph Speaks Again to Families

"Dear child,
The sin of the world is tearing at the very fabric of life and families are divided and suffering because of this. The steady decline of morals in society, in America, no longer upholds families but tears them apart. The children are suffering because love of money, material things, prestige and power, has made them orphans. Many families abide in a house as strangers to one another. Too little time is spent together as family. There is alienation and loneliness in families where there should be relationship and unconditional love. The spirit of the world that entices one away from the family is very strong in this age. That is why prayer is so necessary. Prayer is powerful toward avoiding the seduction that surrounds family members. Therefore, pray, pray, pray. Have courage. God is with you. I love you and bless you. (St.) Joseph, His worker"

38. **11-26-96**
The Consolation of Jesus and Mary Along the Via Dolorosa

During the Rosary with Father at my home at the First Decade, the Agony in the Garden, Jesus said: **You, My beloved ones, are My consolation when you echo My words of surrender to the Father. When you say, "Not Mine but Your Will be done", you are consoling this tender Heart of Mine. At a time when pride and disobedience are rampant, the echo of My surrender becomes a soothing salve for the wounds of My Sacred Heart. Not only is it My Consolation, but yours as well. When you surren-**

der to the Father's Will, His Divine Providence leads you in the way of the Holy Spirit which is the way of love, peace, and joy.

At the Scourging at the Pillar decade, Jesus said: **My flock, My sheep, remember always that by My Stripes you are healed! I bore your debt. I am the Good Shepherd who loves you with an everlasting Love that never fails.**

During the Third Decade, the Crowning with Thorns, there was silence.

At the Fourth decade, the Carrying of the Cross, when Father mentioned Mary's union with Jesus on the way of Calvary, Mother Mary responded. *The union of our hearts is incomprehensible to your human understanding. On the way to Calvary, I was united as one heart with my Son experiencing the depth of His sorrow and suffering mystically with Him.*

After some silence, she continued. *Dear children, I am again walking the way of Calvary. I am walking with the Mystical Body of Christ along the Via Dolorosa in the time of the Church's passion. I suffer as the Mystical Body continues to suffer, mirroring the passion of my Son. As the Body suffers, the Mother suffers. As Mother, I offer assistance along the way.*

Dear children, you are well along the way of the Via Dolorosa and I am present to you as I was to my Son, Jesus. My maternal gaze meets your eyes to behold your every tear and I behold your anguish along the way. I see in your eyes the weariness from the journey. But as you pray your Rosaries, I see new glimmers of hope in your eyes. And as you receive our Jesus in the Eucharist, I see new strength in you that comes from His Divine Life.

Gaze into my maternal eyes along the road of Calvary and find that my motherly gaze will take you into the consolation of my Immaculate Heart to be fed and nurtured for the journey. Do not bear the weight of your cross alone. Look up from the path you are walking to find that you have my maternal presence beside you and that Jesus is bearing the weight of your cross with you. Know that your angel and the saints are there, stationed along the way to assist you and urge you on to the goal - the glorious goal of union with God. He walked the Via Dolorosa to show you the way to the Resurrection. Walking in His footsteps, you will never be lost. You are found in Him.

My children, you are the Body of Christ, His Church, victorious and His people of the Resurrection. Walk in peace and security. God is with you forever. I love you. Your Mother

39. **12-1-96**
Advent, Preparation, and Contemplation of the Incarnation

During the Rosary with Father, I entered a prayer state, which rendered me unable to hear his meditations. At the end, I heard Our Lady interiorly.

My beloved son and daughter, thank you for praying the Rosary on this first Sunday of Advent. Today marks the beginning of the year dedicated by the Church to my Son, Our Lord and Savior, Jesus Christ. The most important of times had begun for mankind.

Beloved ones, again I invite you to enter more deeply into the silence and holiness of my *Immaculate Heart so that you can enter more deeply into the profound mystery of that holy night of our Savior's birth.*

My Immaculate Heart is your refuge from the world that wants to keep you from entering in the mysteries of God to rob you of the knowledge of how deeply the Father has loved the whole of His creation.

What a profound mystery! What glorious wisdom that Jesus Christ would enter the world clothed in humility, poverty, and hiddeness.

Now is the time when you can prepare and anticipate the Savior's coming again. By the power of the Holy Spirit, He shall manifest His glory for all to see so that on earth the Father's Will shall be done as it is in heaven. Prepare the way for the era of sanctification. Look forward to the restoration of life on earth. Prepare your hearts. God alone should fill you. Purge all that is not of God!

Enter into the silence and holiness of my Immaculate Heart each day of this important Advent season so that I can make your own heart a silent and holy place of rest of our Savior's birth. Let Him be born again in your heart that is prepared and waiting.

Today has begun a time of birthing, a time of transition, a most important time of history. Follow the lead of Christ's Vicar,

Pope John Paul and dedicate yourselves again to the Sacred Heart of Jesus Christ. During the new year (1997) contemplate the mystery of the Incarnation. In Him, you have already received the greatest gift of all!

Pray that you will have a deeper understanding of my Son, Jesus. Pray that you fall in love with the One who is the Source of Love. I am with you especially to assist you to keep this season of Advent, holy. I love you. Your Mother

40. **12-4-96** 8:30AM Holy Mass at Communion and before the Tabernacle
Eat My Body and Drink My Blood!

My creation, My Body is the rich, rich food of the banquet and My Blood is the pure wine of the feast. The banquet is a mystical feast of Divine Love. All are invited. Few accept the invitation. But the few who partake do so to the full and become like the rich food and the pure wine, which sustain the Mystical Body. These become the "sacrament" for other souls.

There are many whose faith in My True Presence has faded away. Woe to those in positions of teaching who sow seeds of confusion and doubt. In this age, there are many teachers who have lost true faith and lead others along a faithless path to believe only in the wisdom of the world. Fear of the Lord, your God, is the beginning of wisdom! Wayward teachers have lost their fear of God and where this is absent, the wisdom of the world enters leading only to folly. O how the wisdom of the world can tickle your ears and move your heart in ways of delight. The human heart gives in so readily to the ways of rationalization and self-satisfaction. But the wisdom of God says, "Deny yourself. Take up your cross daily and follow Me." The wisdom of God is the cross. These words do not tickle your ears or move your heart to ways of delight unless you have the Holy Spirit to teach you the true meaning of these words that lead to eternal life. My Ways are not your ways!

My creation, the Holy Spirit is with you to teach you the way. But He does not violate your free will. He leads you and teaches you at every moment if you but acknowledge Him, accept and desire Him. You are invited to an incomprehensible banquet of Divine Love. But that love comes to you in and through the cross of salvation. Love is an exchange of hearts. I gave to each of you My Sacred Heart of Love when I hung on the cross as ransom for the sin of the world. You pierced My Heart with rejection. But when the sword entered Me, a fountain poured out; a fountain of blood and water. You were baptized in My living water gushing from My pierced Heart. You were covered in My living Blood that you would have life eternal. My Body and My Blood are with you until the end of time. But in this age, the enemy works to spread error, confusion, and doubt about My True Presence in the Eucharist. Why? He doesn't want you to partake of the rich food of My Body and the pure wine of My Blood because you will be transfigured into the One whom you eat. The enemy wants to rob you of the banquet of Divine Love that is meant to be yours. When you eat My Body and drink My Blood, you have My Life in you. Then you are able to discern the Holy Spirit from the evil spirit. Then you have strength to battle for the good and resist the evil. Is it any wonder that the enemy seeks to diminish or eradicate this Sacrament of Love? He knows the power of this Sacrament more than you do.

Love is an exchange of hearts, born in the will; it is a decision. I give to you My Heart and My Life. At every moment, I am yours. All I ask of you is that you give to Me your heart and your life. At every moment, will you be Mine? This kind of surrender to My Divine Will requires the strength, the life that comes to you through the Sacrament of Holy Communion. Eat of the rich food of My Body and drink of the pure wine of My Blood as often as you can. Come to the banquet. Live out your decision to love with the strength that comes from My Body and Blood.

May I, the Lord your God, have your heart, your life? I love you with an everlasting love. Your Jesus

41. **12-6-96** Prayer Group
Toward Restoration – A New Birth

My dear little children,
Indeed, all of mankind is walking the way of Calvary at this time in the history of the world. You are intercessors for the family of man. You must always remember that Calvary led to the salvation of souls. Jesus did not remain on the wood of the cross. He arose to reveal His Glory at the Resurrection. You are living the most important days of Advent leading to the celebration of the birth of my Son, Jesus. But also you are living the days of the birthing of the era of sanctification, the promised time when the Father's Will shall be done on earth as in heaven. All of earth shall experience a new birth. All the preparations are underway.

The enemy cannot thwart God's plan, which calls for the restoration of the family of man. But he prowls the earth at this time to devour as many souls as possible before he is banished. Therefore, you will witness the battle between evil and good continue to escalate over the next few critical years. Though there will be much suffering, there will be more heavenly graces poured upon the earth. You will see the mercy of God in your midst even as His Justice is poured out. You will experience the joy of the nativity as you are made to be like the Child, Jesus – humble, pure, and holy. Enter into the simplicity and purity of that holy night in Bethlehem. You are being emptied out so that in your spiritual poverty you can be made truly rich in grace.

Whatever you are made to give up in the way of sacrifice, suffering, persecution, it shall be made up in grace from God. His grace will enable you to have childlike acceptance of the Divine Will of the Father. You will have grace to have hope that becomes the light by which you draw people to God. You will lead them along the way of holiness. The way is the road to Calvary but it does not end at Calvary. It leads to birth, to the resurrection of a new world. The world as you know it is passing away. In these times you will see it die many deaths. But also you will see new life spring up everywhere.

I am with you dearest children, to assist you to fulfill your ministry. Your ministry is to love and to intercede that all men will have love. Prepare. Persevere. Keep watch. Stay alert. God will manifest Himself soon. As the Infant Jesus is born again this Christmas night, know that His life is born in you also. Through Him the world will have new life and in Him the world will have true peace. I love you and bless you with the oil of my maternal love. Your Mother

42. **12-8-96** Feast of the Immaculate Conception
The Graces of Consecration to The Immaculate Heart

3PM at home, I was alone and knelt before the statues of Our Lady of Fatima and the Sacred Heart in my prayer room. I prayed the renewal prayers of consecration to Mary, the St. Louis de Montfort consecration.

When I completed those prayers, I prayed from the depths of my heart, "O admirable Mother, present me to thy dear Son as His eternal slave so that as He has redeemed me by thee, by thee He may receive me!" Overcome with love for my Mother Mary, I wept and spoke to her like any little child would speak freely to such a loving and attentive Mother.

"Mary, my mother, three years ago I made my initial consecration to your Immaculate Heart. Little did I realize then the power of such a consecration! But through it, having chosen your Immaculate Heart to be the means by which I would go to Jesus, I allowed you, I implored you, to take me along the most direct path to the center of the Heart of Jesus.

"You have done just that! Never have you left my side. You knew that I would falter, that I would embark on wayward paths if left on my own. So you surrounded me with your maternal presence and protection, guiding me on the straight and narrow path, toward my singular goal – the Heart of Jesus, my Redeemer who is Love!

"O Mary, the way of wisdom is through your heart! When I humble myself to become your slave, I am actually raised up into the Holy Family and blessed as if I were royalty also! Knowing the truth of my sinfulness, what relief it is to hide myself as slave inside your Immaculate Heart which is always so pleasing to God, so one with His Divine Will!

"Above all of His creatures, you give Him honor and glory, O Seat of Wisdom, my Mother! Root me ever deeper into your Immaculate Heart, dear Lady, so that with you, I am ever more deeply rooted in the Most Sacred Heart of Jesus. O, how I love Him!

"O Mother, hasten the day that the Eternal Father observes the brilliant radiance of love issuing forth from the Heart of His Only Son and finds me there, His littlest ray of light, shining brightly with love for Him. That is the only way that I can give glory to My Father in Heaven! That is how I will please Him!"

Suddenly, Our Lady said: *Daughter of mine, the Father calls you his little light. He is glorified by the light that is in you already - the Light of the Holy Spirit! You are His little light because you bear witness to His Light. The Father sent Jesus into the world to be Light for the world. As many as received Him, to them He gave the right to become children of God. The Father is glorified by the Light, for with God, there is no darkness. Where the Holy Spirit lives, there is light. The Eternal Father recognizes the light within your soul to be His Own!*

Daughter, thank you for consecrating yourself again to my Immaculate Heart. On this feast celebrating my Immaculate Conception, many graces are poured from heaven to earth for the souls who are open to them. Magnify the Lord with me! He chose my lowliness to manifest His greatness in the perfect plan of salvation through the Word Incarnate who redeemed the world!

Today is a reminder of the perfection of His Divine Providence. Pray with me that all the world will come to believe in Him and come to trust in His Divine Providence. Soon the Just Hand of the Most Holy Trinity will purge the world of its present darkness and all will bear witness to the Light of Love.

In His Divine Mercy, He is once again, raising up the lowly, the poor in spirit, to be His witnesses, to be His light bearers to form the army that will triumph with my Immaculate Heart over the darkness of this age.

In this holy season of Advent, keep praying in expectant faith and have hope for a new springtime for Christianity. Rejoice in the Light. He is with you always. I bless you in His Holy Name. I am your Mother.

43. **12-13-96**
Where Do I Fit, Lord?

During Holy Hour following morning Mass I prayed to Jesus, "Lord, what do you ask of me?" Immediately, I heard Jesus say: **Be My bride! Consummate our love upon the cross. I love you, *Soul.** Then I received an image of myself on the cross with Jesus and together we offered the suffering up to the Father in reparation for sins. Then the image ended.

I prayed to Jesus, "Lord, where do I fit?" I heard interiorly, **In My Church! Your life is in and for My Mystical Body. I love you.** These words brought an infusion of grace and I was filled with love for the Church.

44. **12-13-96 (B)** Prayer Group Meeting
Graces of This Christmas 1996

My dear little children, blessed are you who seek wholeheartedly the Divine Will of the Most Holy Trinity. Blessed are you who have love in your hearts and hearts that are pure. I have prayed with you this night. You have been reminded tonight of the transitory things of this world in the image given to my beloved priest. You have been reminded that all the things of the world crumble away. Therefore, set your whole heart, mind and soul upon the everlasting covenant of love.

Jesus is the rock of your salvation. He alone is your stronghold. Unchanging and never ending is His covenant with His creation. Be not afraid as you witness the world, as you know it, passing away. God will never pass away and in Him you have eternal life. Many are expecting physical signs and tragedies to come upon the world. This will come to pass. But more important are the spiritual signs and tragedies that are in your midst now. The loss of a soul is by far the greatest tragedy of all. Look with your spiritual vision that comes from the Holy Spirit that you may see clearly the things of the spiritual world. The battle you are fighting is a spiritual battle over the eternal life of souls.

Man has lived through many ages and transitions of time. But what marks this transition from all other previous times is that you are living the age that will see the serpent overcome and put into the abyss so as to free the world of his evil presence. You were chosen for this critical time in the history of man. Therefore, as God has chosen you, He will empower you by the power of His Holy Spirit.

When this holy night (Christmas) comes upon the world, all of the earth shall be baptized in the Spirit again. Not that all will accept this now. But that those who will accept it, shall have new strength, new light to persevere in the faith leading others in the way of hope and love.

Pray fervently that many hearts will be opened this holy Christmas night so that God's grace, abundant, alive and new, shall again be born into the world as light into the darkness. My joy is that there are many who shall be blessed. My sorrow is that there are many who shall refuse to believe and in their disbelief shall be led down the path to perdition. Therefore, again, I implore you to be courageous in your faith, hope, and love. I bless you in the name of the Most Holy Trinity. I love you, each and everyone, as if you were my only child. Thank you for your prayers this night. Your Mother

45. **12-17-96** Rosary with Father at my home.
Love: The Glory of God and Means of Transformation and Mary at Pentecost

At the decade of the Resurrection, I saw Jesus appear coming forth from the tomb, resplendent in His glorified Body. Overwhelmed by His brilliant Light and Presence, His beauty captured my soul and I marveled at His glory!

He said: **My glory is My Love! I am Divine Love. Love is My glory. This glory is the union of love in the Most Holy Trinity. I am the Father's glory and He is My glory and the Holy Spirit is our glory and we are His. There is nothing more glorious, more majestic, more sovereign, more omnipotent than Divine Love, always new and alive! Divine Love constitutes My glory and you enter into it whenever you love. Therefore, love and continue to grow in love!**

Suddenly, the image changed to the inside of the tomb, the cave of His burial. I saw Jesus standing behind an altar in the tomb. He was the High Priest celebrating a Mass. He held the Eucharist up to the people now gathered inside. The cave was dark except for the light of the High Priest and the light of the Eucharistic Host, which shone on the people.

Jesus said: **This is the means by which I will draw My people back to Me and to the Father. The Eucharist will bring My people back! I will sanctify My people by this means. All will be restored by means of My Eucharistic Love.**

Soul, the burial site represents the appearance of death, which actually brings forth new life. The cave is a symbol of the deadness, which will prefigure new life on earth. The Mystical Body, the Church, will be transfigured in hiddenness for a time. There will be apparent darkness and then out of the silence, will come a resurrected Body of Christ.

At the decade of the Descent of the Holy Spirit, Mary said:

Dear children,

At the foot of the cross, at Calvary, my vocation became Mother of the Church, Mother of all People and all Nations. This is my vocation until the last soul reaches its destination for all eternity. From the moment of my Immaculate Conception, the Holy Spirit became my Spouse as the Eternal Father willed it. But at the time of Pentecost, I also, experienced a new anointing of the Holy Spirit. Each of us in the Upper Room received new graces to empower us to spread the Gospel and birth the Church on earth. The graces of Pentecost fortified us through the difficult times of the early Church. The power of Divine Love enabled the apostles and disciples of Jesus to lay down their lives for the sake of the Gospel of Love. These were simple and ordinary people but the Spirit within them was extraordinary! The task of the bringing to fruition the birth of the Church was difficult and required great sacrifice, courage, and zeal. And the Holy Spirit provided all that was necessary.

Dear children, pray to the Holy Spirit to enliven you in faith. Pray for a spirit of sacrifice, courage, and zeal. Above all, pray that you may know love and grow in love every day of your life.

Pray for a new Pentecost for the Church, for the world so that all of creation will become a reflection of God's own divine beauty and love. Come into the Upper Room of my heart and pray with me. The Holy Spirit will not disappoint us. He, Himself, is invoking such prayer from you! I love you. Your Mother

46. **12-27-96**
On the Beloved Apostle John and Assistance of Saints

Since Christmas day, my soul is in profound peace. A reassuring calm has come over me. Union, awareness of the Presence of God, is almost constant in a peace of soul that cannot be disturbed. There is a very strong protection from evil attacks on my soul since Christmas Eve. However, physically, I have pain across the shoulders and upper back. Today, Friday, the pain intensifies and feels like fire in the muscles. Because it is the Feast of St. John, the Apostle, I make extra effort to attend the Mass in spite of the pain.

I prayed after Mass. "My dear Jesus, certainly You loved all Your disciples without distinction but it seems that John, the Beloved, was especially close to Your Heart. What endeared him to You that I may imitate?"

Jesus had a very joyful disposition as He said: ***Soul of My Cross, St. John, the Beloved, was completely absorbed in the things of God. Forgetful of self, He had an insatiable thirst for love. He lived his days caught up in the wonder and awe of God with Him. The light absorbed him and He absorbed the light. But what endeared this beloved apostle to My Heart was his awareness, wonder, and dedication to My Mother. He was truly her son. Their union of heart was unique, and always one with the Divine Will. He was the first to practice perfect devotion to Mary. She taught him to "listen." The soul that learns to listen, "hears" the things of God.**

The Light was with him and the Holy Spirit came to him through the heart of Mary Immaculate. John recognized the treasury deposited in her maternal heart. He drew near and withdrew all that he needed, knowing that My Own inexhaust-

ible treasury flows through her heart. She fed him the wisdom of her heart.

John learned love because love was with him. John learned discipleship through the power of maternal love. He grew by imitating My relationship with My Mother after My Ascension into heaven. And through our united hearts, he was raised up high in the mysteries of Divine Love so that he would deposit them into the Church's treasury of truth.

Blessed are you who listen. You will be given to hear the things of God. Blessed are you who come to Me through My Mother's heart. Wisdom is imparted to such a soul and with her you attain heights that would not be possible without her maternal intercession.

Invoke John to assist you to listen and hear. Ask him to assist you to recognize Me always and everywhere. He will help you as he helped the apostles saying, "It is the Lord!"

I thought Jesus was finished with the dictation and I began to gaze at the crucifix above the altar. Jesus said: **Drink, drink, child.** I drank of His precious Blood. It flowed so strongly that it seemed I was gulping to take it in. And I was overcome with joy beyond words. He too, seemed joyful to give to me. It is His nature to love, to nourish, to lavish souls who will accept.

I prayed: "O my God, what a wonder You are!" When the grace ended, I recognized some of the saints who had lifted me up. They were St. John, St. Francis, St. Mary Magdalene, St. Catherine of Siena, St. John of the Cross, St. Teresa and St. Therese, the Little Flower. There were many others whom I did not recognize. But they all formed the ladder by which I could be lifted up to the cross, to draw closer to Jesus to reach His wound of love and drink of His life-giving Blood. "Be glorified, my God!"

47. **12-28-96**
Another Spiritual Battle

All day long, I am battling a storm of evil spirits. I am alone and attacked by a terrible spirit of aversion to prayer, silence, and solitude. Father offers to pray with me over the phone, but I refuse.

I give into the negative thoughts and the spirit of murder (of the spiritual life) seems to overcome me. The cross seems unbearable and hope seems to drain out of me. I sink quickly into depression and desire to compensate for the pain. In the midst of this storm, I tried to read about the lives of the saints, which helped. But ultimately, I had to call Father for prayer over the phone and he bound and cast out the evil spirits. I could not do it alone. How prideful to think that I could.

48. **12-29-96** Prayer Group Rosary. Feast of the Holy Family
The Eternal Father Watching Over Us

During the decade of Jesus' Ascension into heaven, an image was given of God the Father. This image portrays Him sitting on His throne in heaven, shining rays of light from heaven into the room where we are gathered in prayer. He observed us. During the Descent of the Holy Spirit decade, I asked the Father, what do you observe? He said: **I observe a flock of sheep and a good shepherd.** His disposition was joyful. After the Rosary, He dictated this message.

Beloved children, you have been well prepared by the Blessed Virgin Mary to offer intercessory prayer for all souls. I, who am your Eternal Father, bless you as you offer your hearts and prayers. I am glorified by love. I observe that you are before Me for love of Me. I who am your Father claim you for My Own. I am pleased to be with you in an intimacy of love that is beyond your human understanding.

My beloved children, know that you have been well prepared that I may use you in wondrous ways in the most tumultuous days, which are upon you. You are soldiers in the army of Mary, Most Holy. Hers is the army of intercessors, praying, suffering, sacrificing for the conversion of the world. Take courage. The world shall be converted. The purification is at hand. You are chosen to uphold the faith while everywhere, faith will be waning. There is nothing to fear. Every grace shall be yours. Every prayer cenacle shall be raised up to battle against Satan's final attacks. I, your Eternal Father, shall be present to you in

many new graces in the days of the new year. You shall have the Blessed Mother's presence with you to guide you through the trials to come. Look to her Immaculate Heart. Her heart gives Me most glory. Let her heart be your refuge, peace, and strength.

In this year dedicated to My Beloved Son, Jesus Christ, look to His Eucharistic Love to bring back souls. Many lambs who have been lost shall find the way back through His Eucharistic Love.

On this feast of the Holy Family, I bless you because you are together as a holy family. I have given to you, the presence of St. Joseph and St. Mary with the Child Jesus so that you may grow in the holiness they bring to you. Families require sacrificial love. In that sacrifice of love, you are made holy.

Remain as Mary and Joseph remained, in prayer, on bended knee (posture of humility and reverence). Pray that you may walk in humble abandonment to the Divine Will. Their intercession is for every soul. United to their hearts, your intercession reaches every soul. I am the Eternal Father of all creation. I am Love. Bring souls to Me. I love each soul infinitely. Love as I love. Dedicate yourselves to Jesus this year. Pray that you may grow in knowledge and understanding of the Word Made Flesh. In this way, I will be glorified by you. I accept your bouquet of love this night and I bless you with a special gift of fortitude. Be strengthened for your journey. I am with you. I love you. Your Eternal Father

Note: During same Rosary, Father received an image of all the prayers of the faithful (souls) rising like incense from earth to heaven. All around the world, cenacles of prayer form a pillar of incense rising to God. Together our prayers are a great plea from earth to heaven. Come Lord Jesus... soon!

Another image was given of Jesus rising up into heaven. He took with Him the jewels, riches, material goods that had been given to the United States of America as gifts. These were being taken back to bring about a time of stripping away so that our focus would be on God - not material things.

49. **1-4-96**
A Plea for Help

I went away to be alone because I was in so much pain I needed to set myself apart for awhile. I prayed to God. "Eternal Trinity, have mercy upon my poor soul! I am beaten to the ground, falling under the weight of this cross. The enemy of all souls never leaves me alone! And like a sledgehammer to a piece of clay, I am broken into little pieces. There are no consolations. No creature on earth can help me. Only the priest who directs my soul has an inkling of this suffering!

My Triune God, You alone are my refuge but your refuge is in the darkness of faith! How incredibly dark is this night now! Each moment is a torment to my soul; an agony to my mind and spirit. I live moment to moment. In the morning I dare not think what noon will bring; at noon what evening will bring. I know only that it will bring another battle because the enemy is poised on all sides and ready to attack at every opportunity. I am so weary from the battle! Silence is my only protection. It must be your Own Hand that seems to put a lock on my mouth to preserve silence!

Jesus, Eternal Word, You have taken my soul to that hidden chamber of Your holy Heart to teach me the way of the cross. Your passion is unspeakable suffering! Aside from the physical torture, there is the unutterable agony of interior suffering enough to kill except that the Father gives the grace that sustains life.

My Lord, what an infinite abyss of Divine Love You are! O Word Incarnate, God with Me, you have tucked my nothingness into that hidden, silent chamber of Your Heart that I may listen and learn the way of Your passion and know that it is the way of true love that saves.

Because You are the greatest of teachers, You allow me to experience this suffering and cause me to fight against the evil one who is permitted to incite malice and hatred against me. You permitted a hammer to be formed and put into the hands of one close to me so that I could enter into Your passion. You willed union through the cross. And now I am a living echo of Your agony and your passion resounds, alive in my spirit.

All human suffering on earth would make no sense except in union with Your passion, death, and resurrection. Is the mystery of human suffering revealed in the word LOVE? Is it possible to love without suffering? You are the revelation of love for God is Love and You are God. But who can love as You love? To do so is to suffer, to lay down one's life for another. Is it any wonder that human capacity to love is so small?

Eternal Trinity, hear the cries of Your people! Send us the Spirit of Love to replenish our emptiness or we will perish. How long before Love permeates Your creation? How many victim lambs? How much suffering due to sin? Have mercy upon Your creation! How long will You permit the enemy to toy with souls? He mocks You as He takes what belongs to You. Each moment souls are walking away from You and choosing the path to perdition. These souls, created for Your love, will never see Your glory, never enter into Eternal Life with You but will suffer forever in the absence of You. What loss! My Triune God, do You not suffer their separation? If You created us for union with You, do You not suffer sorrow over eternal separation?

Suddenly, Jesus began with power, ***Soul of My Cross! This Heart of Mine is an abyss of Divine Love and love cries out for union. Yes! Love suffers all separation! Grace is given to a soul, but the human will is utterly free to choose! I am the Bridge that spans the abyss between earth and heaven having died to free all of creation. I am in constant intercession for each soul. My eyes are fixed upon the Father but My Heart is fixed upon the family of man. I am the Lover of each soul! The Lover does not capture the object of His love by force! The revelation of My Love is made from the beginning to the end and every moment in between. The Holy Spirit makes it so!**

I hear the cry of My people! Not a tear falls that I do not catch and deposit into My Own Heart. Nothing is in vain. I am He who enters into the filth of mankind's sin to bring Good out of it. The human heart is created with a longing for God but human nature tends toward what is base. That is why the Holy Spirit must enter the natural heart to raise it up into the supernatural. But the pride and confusion of this age is astounding! Mankind insists on resisting the truth of the super-

natural reality, denying Me and breaking every one of My Commandments!

So I invite you to cry out with Me to the Father! Yes! Raise your voices and from your heart, cry out "Mercy!" and "Justice." His Hand is purifying the whole of creation. It has begun. Let all of creation be washed in the purification and made clean. Grace will unveil the lies, the evil. And each soul will be given to decide!

*Soul of My Cross, suffer silently and offer everything for the salvation of souls. I am with you always. I love you. Jesus

50. **1-7-97** Rosary with Father at home.
The Spirit That Breathes New Life

During the decade of the Resurrection, I received the Scripture passage in Ezekiel (37:4-10). "Then He said to me: Prophesy over these bones and say to them: Dry bones, hear the word of the Lord! Thus says the Lord God to these bones: See! I will bring spirit into you, that you may come to life. I will put sinews upon you, make flesh grow over you, cover you with skin, and put spirit in you so that you may come to life and know that I am the Lord. I prophesied as I had been told, and even as I was prophesying I heard a noise; it was a rattling as the bones came together, bone joining bone. I saw the sinews and the flesh come upon them. Then He said to me: Prophesy to the spirit, prophesy, son of man, and say to the spirit: Thus says the Lord God, From the four winds come, O Spirit, and breathe into these slain that they may come to life. I prophesied as He told me and the spirit came into them; they came alive, and stood upright, a vast army."

At the decade of the Descent of the Holy Spirit, I received an image of the globe surrounded by darkness. The dove of the Holy Spirit descended upon the earth in a special outpouring of Himself and seemingly wrapped Himself around the earth. Once it was surrounded and supported by Him, He lifted us out of the darkness into a higher existence of pure light.

At the decade of the Assumption of the Blessed Mother into Heaven, Mary said: *Child, I will help you to rise above all that is happening around you. I will help you to go to the heights in and with God. You are being detached from people and things of the world. This is necessary to free you for God, to free you to do His work, to free you to become the person that He wills you to become, fully alive and joyful in Him. Meditate on these words of wisdom, "God alone." I will assist you to live them. I love you. Persevere.*

Then I saw Mother Mary crying over a certain soul. Her face was buried in her hands similar to the image of Our Lady of La Salette. She said, "I am interceding before God for this soul. Help me. I could see that St. Joseph was also trying to help this soul by shining light into it. Mary said: *Pray with us for this soul. Pray for the Spirit to breathe and cause the hardened heart to "come to life." Our tears become reparation and draw many graces. Please do not grow weary of praying for this soul. Do not give up!"*

51. **1-10-97** Prayer Group
Come to My Heart

My dear little ones,

I, your Lord and Savior, bless you with My Presence because you love Me as few love Me. My Divine Sacred Heart is yours. I come to you with My Heart opened wide. I invite you to come deeper into My Sacred Heart of Love. Do not be afraid. Acknowledge your neediness. Fly unto My open Heart. Hide yourself within this tender, merciful Heart of Mine. While most men spurn My Love, you turn to Me with love. Your hearts are pure. I see that you seek My Love. I see that each of you yearns for My Love. I see that you are hungry and thirsty. I, your Lord and Savior, run to you to satisfy you. I am with you in this place and in this time to grant to you all the love that you require.

O how you soothe My aching Heart! O how I love you in ways incomprehensible! Do not close your heart to love. To love is to be utterly vulnerable. Realize that I, the Lord of the Universe, became vulnerable for you. Come closer to Me, My little ones. I will never turn you away. Many of you are receiving the

grace of true self-knowledge. You are beginning to know yourselves at a deeper level. The light of truth is revealing the truth of your littleness, neediness, sinfulness, and weakness. This grace is a necessary step to crossing the threshold to true sanctity, which is grounded in sacrificial love. The more you know the painful truth of your nothingness, the more you can acknowledge your absolute dependence upon Me. Only then can I truly reign in you. I bring My Majesty to you. I bring My glory to you. You become beautiful in Me. Allow Me to tear down the walls around your heart! When you believe you are most broken, that is when I come to you in the most intimate way. Count on Me. There can be no self-reliance. Trust Me. There can be no fear. You are My beloved. Live in Me. Live for Me. Together, always together, we are glorifying the Father. We are interceding for the world. Union is your goal. Walk in My Presence at every moment. Never wander outside My holy Heart. Let us be as one heart. Only through union with Me can you intercede for the world. Your love is the very power behind your prayers. I receive both your love and prayers with much gratitude. I bless you with a drop of My salvific Blood marking you as My co-redeemers. Strengthen and uphold one another along the way of the cross. I love you. I love your families. Be at peace in My tender Heart of Divine Love. Make it your place of rest. And allow Me to rest in you. Your Jesus

52. 1-11-97
Silence as Weapon Against Temptations

I am bombarded with strong temptations to retaliate against a person who is hurting me. My only defense is silence. It is as if I am being led to the slaughter and remain in silence, which is a supernatural grace from God because it is so contrary to my human nature. It seems that God has shrouded me in His Own Silence and it astounds me. I marvel because it is the opposite of my nature in the midst of a trial in which anger could be justified. This silence is one of the most powerful attributes of God's grace in my soul and a sign to me of His Presence. Silence must be a powerful tool against Satan because he is always tempting me to break it but in spite of these almost violent temptations, silence reigns in me. Today, my human nature is very frustrated by this but grace enables me to remain silent, faithful to God's Will.

Throughout the night I battle against evil temptations which assail my soul to belittle and degrade me. It is a night of torment and I realize that I need the prayers of my spiritual director. When he prayed and cast out the evil spirits, peace came.

53. 1-12-97
Mary Teaches of the Triumph of the Cross

In my prayer room, I heard Our Lady: *Dear daughter, peace of my Son, Jesus, be with you. You do not suffer alone nor is any of your suffering in vain. On the contrary, all of your suffering has merit before God, drawing grace for souls. I weep with you and suffer in union with your family. But I am able to see what you cannot. I see that your soul is more radiantly beautiful because you have grown in virtue through this suffering. The light in your soul is brighter than before. This cross has been a catalyst that has transfigured you into the image of my Son, Jesus.*

You are co-redeeming by the power of His Love in your soul enabling you to endure great persecution and overcome terrible temptations. Dear daughter, if you could see the good of this trial, you would rejoice. God has empowered you through this cross. Do not be discouraged. Be at peace and persevere moment to moment. Focus on Love. Love will take you to the heights. Love heals everything. Love always triumphs. Love is irresistible. Love saves souls. Love unifies, strengthens and endures everything!

Your grief, tears, even your temptations, have value before God! Your love will save many souls. Your endurance of this trial is glorifying God. You are blessed to be chosen for this. And the Heart of the Redeemer is your refuge, your treasury. He has taken you into the deepest chambers of Love. The trial you suffer now has opened the door to His Riches. His Divine Grace is filling your human heart to keep it open to love those who hurt you. Abandon yourself into the hands of the God of All Ages and trust that

He will uphold you against every enemy. He will embellish you to walk upright all of your allotted days. He chose you and you are His! Do not doubt. Rest in His Love. This is the greatest gift of all – His Love for you. Thank you for your sacrifice. Thank you for permitting my maternal love to come to your aid. You are loved. I am your Mother. Trust.

54. **1-12-97 (B)** Feast of the Baptism of the Lord
Baptism!

In the evening after prayer, Jesus began: **Beloved, Holy Scripture records the account of My Baptism and Mother Church remembers it today so that the faithful can embrace the revelation of the Trinitarian Life into which you are baptized also. I, the Son of God and Son of Man, sanctified the waters so that the water of baptism can sanctify each soul. The Sacrament of Baptism is an outward sign of a profound interior reality in the life of a soul becoming the initiation into the Trinitarian life. That Life, true Life in Me, is imparted to a soul in a particular way through its Baptism. Like so many of the Sacraments, people do not realize the magnitude of the gift!**

Blessed are the souls who pray and meditate on the revelation of My Baptism. It is My invitation into Divine Love and Eternal Good.

The Father so loved the world that He sent His Only Begotten Son! (Jn 3:16) The voice of the Eternal Father resounds in the heavens and the earth to reveal to every generation, from beginning to end, "This is My Son! This is the revelation of the Father's Love!" It is Love that dignifies humanity. I, the Eternal Word Incarnate, walked in the fullness of your humanity inviting you into the fullness of the Most Holy Trinity. Be baptized in My Name! Whatever I did during My earthly pilgrimage, I did so that you will imitate Me!

The Holy Spirit rested above My Head in the form of a dove as the Father professed, "This is My Son", revealing that wherever I AM, the Father is also and so too, the Holy Spirit! You are temples of the Holy Spirit who comes to your soul to

bear witness to Me because I am the revelation of the reality of Trinitarian Love. Through the sanctifying waters of baptism, you are initiated into the Life of Divine Love.

Hearts should cry out in gratitude and reciprocal Love! But the Father, Son, and Holy Spirit are met with indifference!

Scripture, Mother Church and her Sacramental gifts are vehicles of sanctifying grace for the life of your soul! The human body cannot live without water. Souls cannot live without the waters of Divine Grace flowing through the sacramental fountain. Blessed is the soul who draws from the fountain! Eternal Life and Infinite Love shall be yours! Draw from Me My creation! All that you required, I AM. I give to you, My peace. I am your Jesus.

55. 1-14-97
United States of America

After Mass and Holy Hour, Jesus began: **Beloved ones, winter will be difficult. Stay alert. Many will look forward to relief in springtime, but spring will not bring relief. It will bring the unexpected. The covenant of Love has been broken by you. United States of America, you are a leader among men. All the nations observe you. But, I, the Lord, cry out, "Justice!" Whatever suffering comes to you will serve to eradicate your pride and greed. I will permit affliction because it will cause you to reach out to one another. I will tear down the walls between you. Barriers will fall as I cause you to come into relationship with your neighbors again.**

The blood of the innocents (aborted babies) will co-mingle with the tears of the guilty as you are made to see what you have done. In the name of freedom you have become a culture of death and no longer do you uphold life. While one hand is busy offering help, the other is busy offering death. And the children who are permitted to live quickly suffer the loss of innocence due to the rampant impurity which is common in society now. Faith is waning. Look around you. People are discouraged to the point of despair. Materialism and selfishness

have not brought happiness. I, the Lord, your God, shall cause you to seek Me again. I am the Sovereign Power over you. I blessed you in abundance; but you have turned from Me. I will cause you to turn back to Me.

Stay alert, but do not be afraid. What happens in your country will serve to call you back to the Truth. The Light will penetrate your spiritual darkness and through suffering, you shall be purified. I will put you on the right path. For I love you with an everlasting love. My Love is mercy and justice intertwined. Stay alert and watch what My Hand brings about! You appear to be prospering. But money cannot remedy the erosion of love causing emptiness of heart.

I will humble you. Then shall I infuse your hearts with new life to bring you back to Me. The fabric of faith has been rent. My Own Hand will repair this. After seasons of purifying and healing, I will restore you and cover you with a garment which shall not be rent. When you repent, the Holy Spirit will come to permeate your land and cause you to fulfill the Father's Will. Stay alert. I am your Jesus.

56. **1-14-97 (B)**
Spiritual Marriage

After a short silence, Jesus began again: ***Soul of My Cross, you have suffered My agony in Gethsemane. Your heart bears the marks of one who has been scourged by betrayal. And you have been crowned with the thorns of mockery, ridicule, and rejection. The evil spirit of malice has attacked and wounded you. You walk the way of Calvary carrying a heavy cross. You have fallen many times along the way. My priest has been like Simon of Cyrene for you. You are close to the hill of redemption. Your former self is about to expire so that a purified self can resurrect.**

When I expired on the cross, those who carried out My crucifixion saw the truth as the heavens opened up and the earth shook and in an instant they know – "Surely, this was the Son of God!" Those who carry out your crucifixion will come

to the Truth. And you will live as one who expired in order to resurrect in Me.

My lamb, you are a victim of Divine Love, drinking of the chalice of suffering. But that chalice is our wedding cup. And nothing compares to the beauty of spiritual marriage. Like all the brides who have gone before you, I shall adorn you in radiant white symbolizing the purified state of your soul. And pearls will symbolize the tears born of sacrifice, while flowers represent the prayer and good works. And each soul that you bring to Me will add to the light of your beauty. Having chosen you for Myself, I fashion you to be a reflection of My Own Heart. I love you and forever will our union be your unutterable joy! Take My peace. I am your Jesus.

57. **1-14-97** (C)
Church

After a period of silent prayer, Jesus began again: **Please pray fervently for My Mystical Body. She must walk the way of Calvary leading to a triumphant resurrection. She has endured the agony in the Garden. She has been scourged from within and without. She is about to be crowned with mockery and betrayal. Her crucifixion will continue and pave the way for New Life. Her members are divided, confused, and weary while there is discouragement among priests, bishops, and cardinals. Pray especially for My Vicar, the holy man, John Paul. His suffering is unspeakable, yet he is like a fortress! Go now in My Peace.**

58. **1-15-97** Rosary with my Spiritual Director, my home.
Light To Illumine Souls

After Father heard my confession, we began to pray the Chaplet of Divine Mercy for a certain soul. Then Father began the Joyful Mysteries of the Rosary. Immediately, I was absorbed in prayer.

Toward the beginning of this prayer time, I saw myriads of angelic beings poised at attention, gathered as a vast army. I understood that they were in heaven. I saw the word, "sentinels." These angels formed countless lines. Leaders stood facing the vast army assembled before them. Every angel held a torch-like candle. The leaders of the army held torch-like candles that were already lit on fire. They proceeded to light the first row of candles. Then the first row proceeded to light the second row. I watched this process and saw that most of them had candles that were lit now. On either side of this vast army were angels with trumpets. The trumpets were ready to be sounded. Then I watched one angel travel from heaven to earth in an instant. The angel proceeded to place the candle of light into one human heart to illumine it. I only saw one angel do this to one human heart. But I understood that each one of these angels would transport their candle of light into a human heart so the human heart is illumined in a new light, the Light of Truth. It seemed each soul on earth would be given the opportunity to view itself as it is seen before God, in bare truth. Not every one would accept it. Some will rationalize it away, but multitudes of souls will accept this grace and there will be many conversions of heart.

I became absorbed in prayer again until the end of the Rosary. I received an image of Our Lady and St. Joseph finding Jesus in the Temple. Jesus was busy teaching in the Temple.

Our Lady said: *My children, you are busy about many things in the world. Some of you seek my Son, Jesus, but many do not. A light shall illumine your heart so that you will see without obscurity or deception, the state of your soul before God. This grace will cause you to realize that you are the temple in whom God dwells. You will see clearly the temple's state of being. Is it fit for God? Every human heart will receive the light of truth. In an instant, this heavenly light will penetrate your being and reveal true self-knowledge along with true knowledge of God's existence. God will cause you to look at your guilt so that He can grant you His mercy and reconcile you to Himself. This is a great gift for the world. All of heaven is prepared for it. It will bring many souls back to God. I will be with you to strengthen you. I love you. Your Mother*

59. **1-17-97** Prayer Group Meeting
Pray for Unbelievers and Lukewarm Souls

Dear little children,

You have been granted Light from the Holy Spirit as you gathered again to pray the Rosary in intercession of the salvation of the world. Grow in appreciation of the grace that comes to you when you pray together as my spiritual family. I am always with you when you pray. Know that the light you receive through prayer is a gift that many souls never receive because they do not pray. You are praying for all those who do not pray and who remain in the darkness of the world's way of thinking.

Your prayers are important for the salvation of souls especially the unbelievers and those lukewarm souls who offend God by their indecision. The Holy Spirit has given you images of hope and a promise of a new springtime for humanity. Have hope in your hearts always. The enemy will try to rob you of three things: faith, hope, and love. I am with you to fortify these virtues which are necessary for you to reach the finish line, to claim your inheritance of eternal life in the Most Holy Trinity. You must pray very much so that your faith, hope, and love are strengthened as the enemy tries to attack these essential virtues.

Continue to offer all of your suffering, temptations, trials and prayers toward intercession for a new springtime, the era of sanctification promised to you. Realize that while you are fortified, most souls are being robbed. There is discouragement and indifference in the world because faith is waning and love is lacking. Invoke the Father to send the powerful Light of the Holy Spirit into souls to illumine them with Truth.

I bless you, little ones. Be strengthened and persevere. Your sacrifice is not in vain. The time is closer than you think that many prophecies will be fulfilled. This is a vital year for mankind, a time of decision. And do not worry about your families. I am taking care of them. They will be blessed through your sacrifice of love and intercession. I love you. Your Mother.

60. **1-22-97**
Culture of Death

Father prayed the Glorious Mysteries of the Rosary. At the decade of the Ascension, I received a vivid image of Our Lady. She was sitting down, holding her face in her hands and weeping. She kept weeping! What a sorrowful Mother!

Then she said: *Dear children, I weep tears of sorrow for you because you have become a culture of death. The precious gift of life is not reverenced. I have gathered so many little souls into my Immaculate Heart who have been denied life on earth because of abortion. And their mothers walk the earth wounded, in need of repentance and healing. And the entire Mystical Body suffers because death is being perpetuated. I weep because you live as orphans, as if Jesus has come and gone and because you have not accepted the Holy Spirit into your hearts or converted your life.*

You need the Holy Spirit to guide you in truth and show you the way to resist abortion and choose life. That is why I implore you again today to open your hearts and pray for a New Pentecost! Pray fervently, dear children! Implore the Father to pour out the Holy Spirit to bring you back to life in Him. You are in grave danger. You need the Holy Spirit to live!

Life is beautiful when lived according to God's law of Love. The present selfish lawlessness perpetuates the culture of death. You are accepting the lie of the enemy of life. Do you not understand the atrocity of aborting life? Can you not see what it is doing to society?

When Jesus ascended into heaven, He promised to send us the Spirit of God who would instruct us and remind us of all that He had taught. He told us to wait in prayer, to gather together and wait until the Holy Spirit descended upon us. Only then could we know and live the Gospel and only then could we be His witnesses to the ends of the earth!

I invite you to make my maternal heart your "Upper Room" and invoke the Holy Spirit to be your Light to govern your life in wisdom from on High. Only in the Holy Spirit will you know the truth and preserve the gift of life for all! If you persist in offending God by denying life, you will suffer terrible consequences for your choice against God's law of love. Thus do I weep for you. You are denying God and sin. Will you not come into my Heart and allow me to help you to choose life? Come pray with me. I love you. Your Mother

61. **1-22-97 (B)**
In the Tradition of the Brides of Christ

Later in the Rosary, I received an image of myself standing alone. Suddenly many saints and angels surrounded me and began to adorn me in a white wedding garment. Someone would place flowers on my hair; another would drape a veil around me. Then I was led to a church, which was prepared for a wedding.

Then the Groom appeared and stood before me. Our eyes met in a gaze of indescribable love. Jesus said: **You are My bride forever in the tradition of all the brides who have gone before you. I am your Eternal Groom. Thank you for your sacrifice of love! I know that you suffer and on My account. I find your offering pleasing. I am with you now that you may know in the depths of your heart that you have not suffered in vain. I called you out of the world and you obeyed Me. I stripped away your pride and self-reliance and caused you to rely on Me. I set you apart for Myself and you did not run from Me. You were willing to be a fool for Me and follow My Will in spite of people's opinion or worldly respect.**

My bride, whatever you have lost on My account, is nothing compared to what you have gained. I want you to know that I appreciate your sacrifice. And I graciously accept you in the manner that I have accepted the saints, the brides, who have gone before you and in whose footsteps you follow. We are wedded eternally in a joy beyond your understanding on earth.

Never doubt My faithfulness! I love you with an everlasting love. And you shall bear much fruit for the Mystical Body. The work you give to the world will gather souls unto Me. This is your gift to Me. I accept you into My holy household and bless with the oil of Divine Love. Know that I am with you. Trust Me. I am your Lord and Savior.

62. **1-31-97** Prayer Group
The Spirit of Blockage

Dear children,

Be at peace in the love of God that is in you. You have experienced the spirit of blockage tonight so that you taste of the blockage that exists in so many hearts.

Blessed are you, dear children, because you are open to the gifts of the Holy Spirit. Unite with my Immaculate Heart, the storehouse of the Holy Spirit, so that together we can implore heaven to pierce the hearts of unbelievers and those who are closed to the Holy Spirit.

Your prayers are vital. Through the power of the Holy Spirit the remnant shall unite to call down the rain of God's grace so that hearts are moved to faith in God. This is a very particular time for mankind. Do not allow the enemy to block or distract you from what you are called to be for God. You are called to pray so that you will have love. Be aware of the enemy's tactics of distraction and discouragement in prayer. Prayer is never futile. The spirit of the world will tempt you to think that it is a waste of time. Satan does not want you to pray. He need not attack unbelievers. He is furious with those who have united in my Immaculate Heart, because in them there is power to call down grace to convert many souls.

My heart is pierced with pain for those who do not yet believe in my Son, who do not yet acknowledge the Father, who do not yet accept the Holy Spirit. These souls suffer and walk a dangerous path. God desires not one of them be lost.

Your suffering is in intercession of those who do not have faith, hope, or love. Suffering is temporary and borne with love, leads to eternal life. But the unbelievers suffer separation from God.

Thank you for accepting the way of the cross for the sake of souls. Always seek the Holy Spirit. He is your constant guide shining His Divine Light to illumine the way for you. Seek wisdom! Allow God to be your strength. You shall have the victory of Jesus for yourself and your families who will come to know and serve Him.

You are very little. God loves to use little ones. Be aware of the spirit of intimidation. In your country, you shall be made to feel like fools for believing in Jesus and the Gospel of Love. But you *shall never be put to shame. Remember the words of Jesus, "**In the world you will have trouble, but take courage. I have conquered the world.**" (Jn 16-33) Satan will tempt you in many ways especially to block the graces of the Holy Spirit. Learn to recognize the spirit of blockage. In the name of Jesus take authority and cast it out from you. There is power in Jesus' name and every evil spirit must flee. I will always help you. I love you. Your Mother*

63. **2-5-97** Rosary with Father, 3PM, my home.
Surrender

As Father led the Glorious Mysteries, I saw and heard the following. I received an image of a roaring bonfire. Jesus said: **The Fire of the Holy Spirit is alive and increasingly abundant. The fuel of the fire is Divine Love. Fire will consume the darkness of the world. Fire will provide the light. Do not be afraid of the fire. It brings life.**

The next image was the devil in a court jester disguise. He smiled, then laughed in a hideous outburst of continuous laughter. He was spinning the globe of the world around and around, balancing it on the tip of his index finger. The globe spun like a top. It was shrouded in darkness and he took glee in this.

Quickly this ended when Our Lady put her heel down to crush him. With her presence came gentle reassurance of a sure victory and an overwhelming sense of hope. She said: *Prayer and sacrifice form the lever that presses my heel to the serpent's head.*

Next came a very vivid, evil temptation which I rebuked, calling on St. Michael and it ended instantly.

The next image was one of Jesus on the cross at Calvary. I was prostrate at the foot of the cross. His Precious Blood and Water covered me. I was praying for His Mercy in regards to recent offenses.

After observing this scene for awhile, Jesus spoke: **My bride, victim and lamb, I love you with an everlasting love that does not change according to your merit. You merit nothing. I give as gift My ever present Divine Love. You are worn from the battle.** (Here I had an image of myself in a boxing ring, sitting in the corner during time out and covered with blood from the blows of the enemy, my opponent.) When this image ended, Jesus continued to speak but not from the cross as He had come down. Now we walked along a road together, similar to the scene "On the Road to Emmaus." He was resplendent in His glorified state and I walked in the white garments of a bride.

He continued: **My lamb, when you think you are far from Me, know that I am at that moment closer than ever before. I am pleased with your offering. You are never alone. I uphold you. Obedience pleases Me. Your struggle is known to Me, for there is nothing hidden from My sight. My lamb, appreciate with all your heart and give thanks always for the gifts of the Holy Spirit. Invoke Him to guide your step, to help with every decision. Only in His grace can you decide for Me. Woe to those who stifle the Holy Spirit.**

If you limit the Holy Spirit, you limit My Hand and block the flow of grace, which does not violate a soul's freedom. If you do not desire it, it shall not be given unto you. Grace flows according to your "yes." Hesitation, indecision, fear, and doubt are like a stricture around your heart cutting off the flow of life giving graces. The more constant your "fiat", the more constant the flow of grace.

My lamb, surrender unto My Almighty Arms. Allow Me freedom! I am trustworthy. The faithfulness you seek is found in Me. I will never forsake My covenant of Love with you. I seek to use you for My glory and for the sake of My Mystical Body but you must decide to never place a limit on the Holy Spirit, granting Me the freedom to make you My domain and to use you as My vessel. Do you grant Me this? Yes, Jesus, I do.

Know that your "fiat" is uttered by the power of the Holy Spirit, without whom you could not utter My Name. There is no wound inflicted upon your heart that does not bleed for the sake of co-redeeming souls. And there is no wound inflicted upon your heart that is not healed by My Own (Heart). We are one Heart, bleeding in intercession for the world. The Father's loving gaze is upon us granting grace through our intercession. Do not be afraid of where I lead. It is holy. Know My plans for you are all for Good.

We have shared the cup at Gethsemane; been scourged by betrayal; crowned with rejection and indifference; walked the way of the Via Dolorosa carrying the heavy cross of sin; nailed to the wood for the sake of love; and now you are with Me in the tomb having expired only to rise again. You are waiting for the dawn of the Resurrection. It is close at hand. Patience, My bride! Patient endurance wins the prize of Life Everlasting.

Silence is the shroud that protects you. Be hidden in Me. The victory is assured. Frustrate the rebel (devil) by conforming your will to Mine at every moment. You belong to Me. That is why he targets you. You are the weakest of souls, but I am your strength. Rely on Me. Allow Me freedom without fear. Love Me as I love you. Forever, soul? Forever, Lord!

64. 2-5-97 (B)
Jesus Addresses a Priest

Please tell My priest, "Conform your way to Mine and persevere in strong faith. Love upholds you, therefore, You shall not falter. Do not doubt My Presence. Acknowledge the gifts in your soul without fear, secure in the knowledge that Love is the giver. The hour when every man must decide is close at hand. Prepare My people, praying always for their sake. In sharing the cup of suffering, you share in My glory.

Thank you for interceding for that certain soul. He is important to My plan and you are freeing him from the snare of the hunter for My Glory, for the salvation of his soul. Your prayer is not in vain though you see no evidence. Trust in the way My Hand works. In the end, great good will come out of much suffering. Keep your eye on Mine, your heart in Me. Your consecrated hands bless My House. Be pure of heart and I shall reward you.

Remember to whom you belong, forsaking your former ways, walk upright as one created anew. Bear witness to My grace in your soul, enriching those to whom I send you. My priest, you are tasting of My Goodness, partaking of the

Father's Banquet. Be fortified by My Blood and alleviate your thirst by My Water. Imitate Me! Pour yourself out for others and fortify My Mystical Bride with Love. I bless you in the name of the Most Holy Trinity. I love you. You are like (St.)Peter in your love and service of Me. You are like (St.)John in your love and service of My Mother. You are like the prodigal son embraced by the Father. I give unto you, My Peace, My Love. Your Jesus

65. **2-7-97** After Holy Mass, Exposition of the Blessed Sacrament in Church
Image of the Parting of the Red Sea

Following Holy Mass, I entered contemplation before the Blessed Sacrament. After forty minutes, I suddenly became distracted about family matters. While praying to stop the distraction, I was given the following image.

I saw vividly an image of the parting of the Red Sea, which took place at the time of Exodus when Moses led the Israelites out of slavery from Egypt. There was a group of modern day people being led through the parted sea, which formed a wall on either side of them. I observed this for a few minutes and then heard Jesus speak.

My people,

I, the Lord your God, will lead you out of the bondage of your sin, the slavery of the enemy. The same Spirit that descended upon Moses to empower him to lead My people out of slavery will descend upon you so that you are led out from the darkness of this age. Blessed are you who have heard and accepted the plea from heaven sent to earth through the Most Holy Virgin Mary. Blessed are you who have heard the trumpet sound, blown by the angels that accompany her, to awaken you from your slumber. She was sent by the Father, not speaking in parables, riddles, or complicated language, but speaking in simple terms, the need for you to rise toward God. When she speaks of prayer, when she implores you to con-

vert, she is indeed calling you to rise toward God. You who have heard and responded in humble obedience will have My Spirit to lead you, going before you to overcome all obstacles so that you are delivered from the darkness of this present age and led into a promised land bathed in the newness of springtime.

I prevailed over the hardheartedness of a nation, a people, using their own hardheartedness to bring an end to their oppression of My people. The very spirit of Moses, My humble and obedient servant, is imparted to the heart of My Vicar on earth. Moses said to the people, "Do not fear! Stand by and see the salvation of the Lord which He will accomplish for you today." (Ex. 14:13) My Vicar echoes these words, urging the faithful to believe and hope, urging the unbelievers to accept the truth of Christianity. I, the Lord your God, am the deliverer. I fought for you, shedding My Blood to deliver you in all ages from all evil. I, Myself will lead you out by the power of My Holy Spirit, anointing leaders with the very spirit of Moses that you will come to safety into a Kingdom that is the fulfillment of the Our Father Prayer, which I gave to you that all would pray in union, throughout every age, "Thy Kingdom Come, Thy Will be Done on Earth as it is in Heaven." Stand by, My people, and pray unceasingly for the coming of that promised Kingdom.

Pray in union with the Immaculate Heart of Mary, more pleasing than any other created by God, because of her humility and obedience. Within her heart is the family, My faithful ones, chosen to be lights unto the nations, through whom all will come into the Light by the power of intercessory prayer born of the breath of My Holy Spirit and able to overcome every other spirit that is not of God. Stand by in faithful silence, like the Lamb who took away the sin of the world, you will be made a holy sacrifice, through whom many will be brought unto the Altar of God and there, find the way to eternal life in Me.

It is easier for Me to command the sun, moon, stars, and seas than to change the hardheartedness of a people because the sun, moon, stars, and seas exist under My Command while man is left free to decide for or against My Commandment of Love. How great is your dignity, My people. But how low you have stooped, forgetful of My Commandments, forsaking My Way for yours and making yourselves obedient to no authority except yourselves. Stand by. It is time for change. Will you follow My appointed leader, My Vicar on earth, into the promised kingdom recognizing that My Spirit is upon him granting him the Authority to part every obstacle? Or will you be swallowed up by the sea of evil? Decide. Accept My Grace. I love you. Your Jesus.

66. **2-11-97** Feast of Our Lady of Lourdes
Our Lady of Lourdes Helps

It was Father's day off so he offered Mass for today's feast at our home and we prayed the Rosary afterward. As we began, there were many temptations, but I persevered in prayer and they ended.

At the end of the Rosary, Our Lady said: *Soul, my daughter, Do not be afraid and do not worry. I am with you.* There was a pause. Then I heard again. *Do not be afraid and do not worry. I am with you.* Again, a pause. Then, *do not be afraid and do not worry. I am with you.*

67. **2-12-97** Ash Wednesday
Transitory Life on Earth

Following Mass and a very graced Holy Hour, I went home and worked at my desk. I heard Our Lady: *My child, pray that you will always be very little. May the ashes on your forehead remind you of the transitory life on earth. It is all passing away! But the love in your soul will never pass away. Pray to be little because the smaller you are, the more God will use you for His glory.*

68. **2-14-97** Prayer Group
Intercede and Have Hope

My dear little children,
Thank you for persevering in your prayers. We are together interceding for the grace of conversion for all souls. Because there is little faith, hope, and love in the hearts of mankind, there exists, fear, anxiety, discouragement and many emotional sicknesses. As the world turns away from its Creator, it becomes sick. You will witness increased physical illness and more emotional illnesses. That is why I implore you to pray unceasingly. Make your life a prayer. Intercede with prayer and sacrifice so that hearts will be converted, becoming well through faith, hope, and love.
This Holy Season of Lent, meditate on the Passion and Death of my Son, Jesus, but always meditate on the Resurrection as well. This will help you to increase in the great virtue of Hope. Only through much prayer can you be instruments of hope for the world. There is too little hope in the world today. It is the work of Satan to destroy man's hope in God. There can be no hope without faith in God. As faith is dying in the world today, so too, is hope. Man's self reliance leads to despair because there is only one reliable One and He is God. Where there is pride, there is self-reliance. Only the humble acknowledge dependence on God. The humble depend on God and in faith, He is their Hope. Your littleness (humility) brings hope to the world.
It would be most pleasing to my Immaculate Heart if you would offer the fifteen decades of the Rosary daily during Lent. I can do so much through your praying the Rosary toward the conversion of souls. I am with you every step of the way and I will continue to teach you. I help you along your journey, individually, and collectively. Turn to your Mother's Immaculate Heart and I will embrace your every burden, taking them to my Son. Together we intercede for you. Bring everything to us. Jesus is at the right hand of the Father in constant intercession of every soul. Praise the Lord, your God. He has done great things for you. A grateful soul draws more grace. Thank you for suffering for the sake of the salvation of souls. Your intercession is not in vain but gains merit for souls who do not know God's Love and do not know peace that comes from prayer. I love you. Your Mother

69. **2-17-97**
The Creator Will Humble Mankind

At my home during the Rosary with Father, I received an image of a very high mountain in a pastoral setting. Suddenly, it was cut in half horizontally, dramatically cut down in size. Then I saw tall business buildings cut in half. Our Lady said: *My daughter, the mountain represents mankind who has raised himself up like a monument. Like a mountain that stands majestically over all its surroundings, mankind tries to stand over the world as if he is the master of all. But the Creator will cut him down to size. Then will mankind behold His Majesty and the truth of man's weakness will be revealed for all. Pray with me.*

Then I saw the globe of the earth as from the heavens. It looked very small in its position in the universe. I observed the globe wrapped in strands of jewels, gaudy in appearance. Suddenly, the globe was cracked open. It was hollow inside – nothingness! On the outside it appeared fully adorned, but inside there was nothing. Our Lady said: *Only God can fill the void. Pray with me!*

70. **2-17-97 (B)**
Admit Your Woundedness and Be Healed

There was a long pause and then Our Lady's presence intensified. She approached me and led me into a pastoral setting like a beautiful expansive garden. Without letting go of my hand, she went to a blackboard just as a teacher would do to instruct a pupil. She was extremely kind, gentle, yet firm, expressing immense maternal love. I truly was her child! She instructed me to look at myself. And somehow I was made to view myself.

What I saw was extremely painful in its truth. I was a very wounded human being. Countless arrows covered most of my being and I did not want to behold this, to admit the extent of my woundedness. But truth prevailed and I had to face it.

How prideful! I still wanted to believe that I was not a wounded person. Our Lady continued to teach me that this woundedness could not be healed by any human consolation. Nothing of the physical world could heal me. In fact, if I sought consolation of the physical world, it would only increase my woundedness. She said: *Only God can heal your wounds, dear daughter. Live in the Holy Spirit and He will heal you by the power of Divine Love.*

I saw clearly my great need of love in order to be well, whole. And Mary said: *What is needed is Love. What is needed is more prayer to open your heart to receive more Divine Love, which heals.*

At the end of this grace, I asked Our Lady about the conversion of a certain soul. She did not respond. But her silence spoke clearly to me and I understood that she was asking me to trust in what God had already promised.

71. **2-19-97**
The Pope's Suffering and Victory

During the Rosary with Father, I received an image of Pope John Paul's heart being pierced with a huge sword. Then I saw the word "martyrdom" and understood that it was spiritual martyrdom, a suffering no less than physical martyrdom.

The image changed to include St. Peter on his right and St. Paul on his left. And before him was St. Ignatius of Antioch who was martyred in Rome, ground in the teeth of wild beasts. I understood that the Holy Father's sufferings will increase in the future and that there are many attacks targeted at him. Later, I saw him in the heavens above St. Peter's Square in the rank of all the martyrs who went before him.

Later in the Rosary when Father prayed for the first book of messages just published, I saw an image of someone sowing seeds along a pathway. The person carried a stack of books but as he tossed them to the wind, they burst into a thousand little seeds that fell to the ground to grow into new life.

During the decade of the Assumption of Mary into heaven, when Father prayed about Mary's pierced heart as she walked the Via Dolorosa with Jesus, my heart was pierced so that I could be in union with Mary's pierced heart.

During the Coronation decade, I saw the word "dogma" and understood it to refer to the fifth and final Marian Dogma proclaiming Mary as Co-Redemptrix, Mediatrix, and Advocate. I saw a golden thread that was being interwoven into new fabric that was abundantly beautiful. This dogma is that golden thread that ties so many graces together for the entire world.

72. **2-19-97 (B)**
The Triumph of the Two Hearts: Man Responds to God's Love

As Father prayed the closing prayers of the Rosary, I saw Our Lord Jesus radiantly beautiful in all white as He walked down a pathway. In His arms were people. And there were more people hanging onto him, to His garments, so that as He walked, He carried them along. Many more little ones followed behind Him.

Next, I saw Our Lady radiantly beautiful in dazzling white garments. She also carried many people in her arms. And more people hung onto her garments as she walked a step behind her son, Jesus.

Suddenly, the focus became the heart area of the people. These little ones had a transformed heart. I could peer into each heart and see that they were pure and filled with God's Light. Each had the dove of the Holy Spirit inside of them.

I somehow saw that for these little ones, it was natural to follow Jesus and Mary. It seemed effortless, like breathing in and breathing out. The joy was indescribable; the fruit of the fullness of the Holy Spirit in each transfigured heart. It had to do with the reconciliation of man to God. God led, the creature followed. The Divine Will became the center of each human heart. The Holy Spirit was alive in the hearts and bore witness to the Love of the Most Holy Trinity. Hearts had responded to God's Love. All of this was directed toward the Eternal Father. His Own were returning to Him. Jesus and Mary led them back. The Two Hearts triumph as the Holy Spirit fills the hearts of the people.

73. **2-25-97**
Continue the Rosary Crusade

After Mass before the Tabernacle, I was praying for my family when suddenly I received an image of many churches with multitudes of people walking away from them. Jesus said: **Pray. The apostasy is underway!**

I continued to pray. Then I heard God the Father. **My child, not much longer will I observe My children walking in this direction.** An image accompanied His words in which multitudes of people were walking away from God, their backs turned from Him. Later when Father and I prayed the Rosary, I was given an image of the globe of the earth surrounded with light that came from the Communion of Saints which is theirs from the beatific vision. I understood this to be a gift for us, the Church on earth. They aid our souls very much. They live!

Then I saw Our Lady holding up a Rosary as she said: *Rosary Crusade.* And she continued: *My beloved children, my Rosary Crusade which began at Fatima has formed a family of little souls united in the Upper Room of my Immaculate Heart. I implore you, little remnant, continue to pray the Holy Rosary for the salvation of the world. The hour of decision is close at hand.*

Do not be discouraged because you are a minority. Through the power of the Holy Rosary a few gain victory over the many. The graces of the Holy Spirit flowing from God through my heart into yours are more powerful than the multitudes that have locked the Holy Spirit out of their lives. The spirit of the world occupies so many hearts.

Your prayers are vitally important at this critical time in history. Take up your Rosaries in this last Rosary Crusade that will bring forth the triumph of the Two Hearts as Satan is crushed and banished. A glorified Church, a resurrected world, will be restored to God's order, reconciled through the power of Love.

You who pray the Rosary with me are the lambs, the sacrificial offerings, saving the souls of many who would otherwise perish. You will be fortified by continuous grace from the Holy Spirit to fight the battles of the final hour, the war waged against the evil of this time. Love is the all-powerful weapon. Pray daily that you grow in love for God. Love will uphold you and make you stead-fast against the devil. Your prayers are more precious than pure gold. Prayer beautifies you because it takes you into the Heart of Our Redeemer. In Him, you are transformed by Love becoming His Reflection.

Do not give in to the temptations of fear, anxiety, and discouragement. Fight the temptations to rest, to cease praying, to doubt and hesitate. You are my army of little saints. Take courage and battle against the spirit of the world that wants to rob souls of grace. Do as the Saints who went before you have done. Persevere to live and spread the Gospel. You are not foolish to pray, to repent, to convert again, to hunger and thirst for Love, to seek His Divine Will. You are wise to do these things.

If you pray, you will know Love. If you love, you will stand with God and will not be afraid even as you witness the apostasy, division, upheaval, and confusion in this final hour between the Woman Clothed with the Sun and the serpent whose head shall be crushed. Your prayers are the lever, the power that will put my heel to his head and crush it.

I love you, little remnant. You are beautiful lambs in the image of the One Unblemished Lamb. To Him be all honor, glory, and praise. Remain united in my Maternal Heart and I will nourish you and keep you safe for God. Your Mother

74. **2-28-97**
Identify with the Lamb of God

At Mass, Satan bombarded my soul with terrible temptations. However, after Holy Communion, the temptations ceased and I entered contemplation.

On the drive home I heard Our Lady. *My daughter, please write for my prayer group.* (Our Lady's disposition seemed "possessive" about the prayer group.) After helping my son, I went to my prayer room and began to pray the decade of the Descent of the Holy Spirit. I received an image of Our lady at our prayer meeting. She put her finger to her pierced Immaculate Heart and drew a drop of blood. She put her finger to the forehead of each person and blessed us with the blood in the form of a cross saying, *In the name of the Father, Son, and Holy Spirit, I bless you as lambs of God.* When everyone had been blessed, she remained in the center of the room. Angels surrounded her.

My dear little children,

Listen and let it penetrate your hearts, please. You do not yet understand who you are. You are struggling with your identity. Allow your mother to teach you, please. You have been called to identify yourself with the Lamb of God who takes away the sin of the world. You are invited to live the spirituality of the Lamb. The time has come. You must decide if you accept the invitation. You are to recognize the call now. Open you heart fully. Do you recognize yourself in the spirituality of the Lamb? You have been led and formed by the Two Hearts that are One Heart (Jesus and Mary). *You have been called to be the lambs, the little flock within the Church that prays and suffers with zeal to take away the sin of the world.*

Little ones, do not look at yourselves to find your identity. Look at the Lamb of God, my Jesus. In Him is your identity, your calling and mission. Each one of you is a little child in great need. Out of your very neediness, the Holy Spirit has given birth to your giftedness. You have not yet understood that it is your littleness, your nothingness, that is your giftedness. This is what you bring to the Body of Christ, a childlike surrender and dependency upon God.

Born of this is humility, obedience, and purity of heart. This is precisely what the Mystical Body of Christ needs today – to be permeated with LOVE born in the heart of a childlike soul! In such a soul, the Holy Spirit lives, bringing true gifts of Wisdom, leading the soul to sanctity of the One Unblemished Lamb of God, the Word made Flesh. He takes away the sin and overcomes the spirit of the world on Calvary. There with Jesus, you also, co-redeem souls. This is the kind of Love to which you are called.

Do not be afraid. Being called by God, you also will be empowered to fulfill the call. I am with you to help you to recognize the call, to respond and fulfill it. Grace will lead you. It is for you to exercise your free will. You must give your "fiat." Pray for one another because you need one another to be well and whole. To-

gether you can answer the call more fully. I pray for you and I love you. Your Mother

75. 3-2-97
Never Degrade Yourself

I began to pray the Chaplet of Divine Mercy in my prayer room at home when I heard Jesus. **My bride, *Soul of My Cross, please do not hurt yourself again. Do not degrade yourself. You belong to Me. I carry you in My Innermost Sacred Heart. When you put yourself down, you put the Lord, your God, down also. I am He who lifts up the soul. Never do I oppress or degrade a soul.**

Know the enemy. Know yourself. Know your God. My Love uplifts. You are more precious to Me than you can comprehend now. You are Mine forever and beautiful in My Sight. Cling to Me in your pain. We are one. Yes, *Soul? I replied, "Yes, Lord."

Jesus continued: **You are the target of the enemy because you are working to spread the truth of My Divine Mercy. You are augmenting My Church. Satan wants to hide the works of Divine Mercy. He wants to thwart forgiveness and reconciliation. He works to divide through unforgiveness. He despises My Mercy. Trust in Me. I will bless your endeavors to spread the message of Divine Mercy. Thank you for your obedience.**

The Church is embracing My Call to Mercy. Through efforts of My Vicar (Pope John Paul) the entire world will come to know of the trumpet that sounded through a simple nun (Blessed Faustina). She was the herald of My Mercy for this critical age in need of Mercy. And through the apostles of Divine Mercy, many will come to the fount of Mercy and drink of My Living Water and Precious Blood to be healed of sin, and Mercy shall bring them back to Life.

You are especially targeted by the devil when you work toward the proclamation of Mary, Co-Redemptrix, Mediatrix, and Advocate because the devil despises this movement which proclaims the whole truth about Mary because he is set against the Woman Clothed With The Sun. He knows of the powerful

graces which will come through Mary and the definition of her maternal roles. He knows of the reward for the Church, for all peoples, because he sees how Mary unifies her children, which is opposite to his seeds of division. Be vigilant when you are working for this movement because it will bring retaliation against you and My priest.

You and Father must pray more than ever. There is much for you to accomplish toward the salvation of souls. Persevere in your work for Me. You are attacked at this critical time because Satan wishes to divert your mission of sacrificing and interceding for souls, for the Church. The more time that you invest in prayer, the less susceptible are you to Satan's attacks. He will continue to assail your soul and attack Father as well.

Now is not the time to rest. You are living in a very important time when you are about to birth work, which will bear much fruit. More than ever, focus on Me. Focus on My Face, My Eyes, My Heart and burn with Love for Me. And I will give you to burn with charity for souls. Do My Father's Will with zeal for His House. Cling to Mary, Spouse of the Holy Spirit, so that you can receive every grace and gift from Him. Be fortified and fulfill your Mission of Love.

You are My bride, My lamb, My altar and in you, I am. I am yours, in you, with you, around you, thoroughly permeating you for the glory of My Father, for the good of countless souls in need of help. Therefore, My beloved one, drink of Your Savior and do not listen to the spirit of the world. Do not listen to the liar. You are no longer of the world. Come now. My Heart is your home forever. Come be with Me in silence, the language of true love. Yes, *Soul?

"Yes, Lord. Forever yes, Lord. Thank you, Jesus."

76. **3-5-97**
The Docile Lambs Will Stand

In prayer at my home, I received an image of Our Lady standing over a little lamb with her arms outstretched in prayer. Suddenly, I observed the lamb's legs being pulled out from under and it fell down. I watched as the lamb was pulled and stretched in many different directions without breaking apart. The lamb was extremely pliable, able to withstand the attack and test. Mother Mary fixed her eyes on the lamb and never ceased to pray in intercession of it.

She said: *My little ones, the remnant is like this lamb. My faithful little lambs are pliable, docile in every situation. The attacks of the devil strike but do not break. God tests to stretch and strengthen your resolve to persevere in the way of littleness, in the call to Love, in the mission of reparation, for the sake of God's plan of salvation. The little flock knows the Voice of the Good Shepherd and He lives in the center of your hearts.*

Beloved children, the Good Shepherd seeks more little lambs. Gather together and pray that the Voice of the Good Shepherd will be heard around the world, calling everyone to come! Come apart from the spirit of the world. Come home, dear children. Come home to God. He alone will satisfy your need. Come to Him and forsake false peace for True Peace found in the Heart of Our Redeemer.

Soon, my little lambs, the world shall receive a grace that springs from the depths of the mercies of the Most Holy Trinity. And many will come to Life. Pray fervently and suffer courageously. Your docility to the Holy Spirit will be your strength and protection. When others fall, you will stand. Blessed are you who receive my words and believe. You will be prepared for the future.

Pray for those who do not believe because they will suffer very much. They have no rock, no foundation, and no pillar of strength to cling to. You will be called to assist these souls. You may be their rock, their Jesus. The Christ in you will be their saving help. Trust. Your Mother watches over every soul with great love and protection for all. Praise the Most Holy Trinity with gratitude for allowing me to be with you today. I love you. Your Mother

77. **3-5-97 (B)**
Let There be Light and Life to the Full

During the Rosary, Father stopped because he was being assailed by temptations. Suddenly, I received an image of his chest as a blackboard and fingernails (evil spirits) began to scratch the blackboard to annoy and disturb his prayer. He bound and cast out the evil spirits and they left.

I also received an image of the Hand of God the Father in an image similar to Michaelangelo's painting of the Finger of God creating mankind. His Finger slowly descended upon the earth in a deliberate and gentle manner. The Father said: **Let there be Light,** which echoes His first words of creation. When He said this, a heavenly Divine Light illumined people's hearts. The Father's disposition was joyful. It was all Good. The Father's joy was to give the gift and observe the fruits; hearts awakened and bathed in New Light which clothed minds and hearts in the Truth of God.

Then the Hand of the Father enveloped the earth, which appeared to be in darkness. The Father uttered the words, **Let there be purification.** The Father enveloped the earth in the palm of His Almighty Hand. I understood that He would allow a time of purification for creation. And He said: **Purification will bring forth New Life.** Then the Father opened His Almighty Hand and Light enveloped the earth, which had changed. He said: **Let there be springtime.** The earth rested in the palm of its Creator, bathed in the newness of springtime. It was full of the Life of the Most Holy Trinity. People knew who the Creator was and they loved Him and served Him. There was reconciliation between God and man. Love reigned.

The Father was delighted in His transformed creation. He saw the image of His Son, Jesus, inside souls. He saw that people's hearts were open to the Holy Spirit and His Gifts, which were distributed abundantly among the people. God the Father was glorified in all of this and said: **Let there be faith, hope, and charity. Let there be Life to the full.**

Re: St. Francis

At the end of the Rosary, I saw St. Francis walking on the earth in the present time, as a beggar, poor, and ragged. He walked as the poorest of poor with hands outstretched and begging. His eyes were full of love and joy. Our eyes met in a gaze of awe and wonder.

He said: "Little dove, pray very much now. I am with mankind by God's grace. I intercede on behalf of the extreme spiritual poverty of this age. The hearts of mankind are like dry deserts. The

Communion of Saints are in your midst to bring fresh living water to souls. I beg everyone to repent and believe in the Gospel! I beg on your behalf before the face of Our Thrice Holy God asking for the greatest outpouring of His Tender Mercy. Pray, little dove. Pray very much. Springtime will come and your suffering will turn into your joy forever. I bless you in His name. I am your brother, Francis."

78. **3-7-97** Prayer Group
Love is Everything!

My dear children,

As your Mother, I desire that you come to know at a deeper level that you are infinitely loved by God. When you grasp the truth of His Divine Love for you, you will have the power of His Divine Love at your disposal. It will be yours to give away because you will be full to overflowing. This is charity for souls born of the Infinite Love of the Most Holy Trinity. Love is the beginning, the middle, and the end. It is time that you descend to the deeper levels of the Most Sacred Heart of Jesus. I will take you there. Together, by the power of the Holy Spirit, you will listen and learn of Love, the Father, Love, the Son, Love, the Holy Spirit. This will fortify your soul with Life! Dive into the very depths of the Word Made Flesh. His Holy Heart is for your exploration. Swim in the ocean of His Divine Love. You will become strong here. Then will you fortify Jesus' Mystical Body (the Church).

The Mystical Body, the bride of my Son, Jesus, suffers very much today. She is in need of restoration. She is in need of faith, hope, and love. You will go to the heart of her and fortify her in the hour of need. I will take you there carrying you in my Immaculate Heart. Together, we will aid in her restoration. Before you can give love away, you must receive love. Therefore, I will take you first to the Heart of Our Redeemer. There you will become full of abundant love so that your fullness becomes charity for others.

Please take to heart my messages. They are for your growth in holiness. Never doubt that you are called to be Holy. Remember, you are made in the image and likeness of God. You are temples of

His Holy Spirit. Walk in the dignity of a child of God. I bless you each individually and collectively. Thank you for your prayers, sacrifices, and love. You are beautiful to behold. I am consoled to observe your hearts that are pure and open. Strive to walk each day in a childlike surrender to God. I love you. Your Mother

79. **3-15-97**
Mary's Blessing

At a conference out of town, I heard Our Lady. *Child, your family is one of many families brought to my Immaculate Heart through this beloved priest.* (My Spiritual Director who was in attendance at the conference.) *He continues to bring souls to my Heart and together we take them to Jesus. Follow where he leads. God can do much more for your soul through the capable guidance of this priest. I bless you both. I am here with you. I love you. Your Mother*

80. **3-19-97** Feast of St. Joseph
Turn to St. Joseph

After Mass and Holy Hour, Jesus said: **My beloved, What a glorious feast day for the Church! Dear faithful, it is fitting for you to remember, to ponder, and draw close to the man whose singular distinction it is to be My stepfather on earth and in heaven, the husband of the Blessed Virgin Mary, St. Joseph!**

He leads the Communion of Saints interceding for souls. He is the patron and guardian of My Mystical Body, the Church. Next to Mary, Joseph shared in the mystery of the Incarnation in ways incomprehensible. Ours is a relationship of a unique union of love.

Today, Divine Light continues to radiate through the soul of St. Joseph onto the whole of creation. Joseph did not leave you a spoken word (in Scripture) **because he desired for you to ponder THE WORD Himself. His silence reveals the attitude of his heart – always listening! On earth he was obedient in**

faith, a model for the disobedience of this faithless generation.

In heaven he is perfected in Divine Love and continues to work toward the salvation of souls as the stepfather of the family of man. O that the world would embrace the ways of this Saint! Behold and ponder the ways of My faithful servant that you may be found worthy when your time comes.

Next to Mother Mary, take Joseph as the example of docility to the Holy Spirit. Rejoice! In the Communion of Saints, you have models who become your teachers by example and your advocates by intercession.

The Father's kingdom is infinite and He is glorified in the unique beauty of each saint. The soul of St. Joseph magnifies the beauty of the Most Holy Trinity because on earth, he listened, obeyed, and loved faithfully. Turn to him and ask that he pray for you to be able to listen, obey, and love faithfully. I love you. Jesus

81. **3-23-97**
Graces and Temptations

During the Rosary with Father, I saw Our Lady holding something in the gathered folds of her gown. She came before us and unfolded the fabric to reveal an abundance of perfect white long stemmed roses. There were countless, rare, exquisite roses. She said: *My children, this represents the graces which I will shower upon you and my priests during this Holy Week as you contemplate the Passion of my Son, Jesus.*

Then I saw a bomb going off in the middle of the prayer group and we scattered every which way. The devil planted the bomb to divide us against one another. Then I saw the image of the Church, which suddenly caved in upon itself. The roof and walls crumbled, but the foundation remained intact. Jesus said: **What man erects will crumble. What the Holy Spirit has built, stands firm forever.**

Then Father prayed for a certain soul and I was attacked by the devil who seemed to shout interiorly, "Unforgivable! Unforgivable!" I rebuked him and the temptation ended. The devil tempts me to anger and retaliation against this soul and I battle constantly to overcome these temptations and continue to pray for the one who has inflicted such terrible pain.

The devil then tempts me to quit the prayer group, causing me to see every member in a terrible negative light and tempting me to the futility of it all. Father prayed over me because I could not be consoled and wept profusely. I was overcome with heaviness and discouragement. Then Our Lady said: *Turn to your Angel of Hope. Hold onto Hope. My child, do not lose hope. Be at peace. I love you and will help you.* Then she showed me the roses again and reminded me of the many graces to be distributed to people as they contemplate the Passion of Jesus this Holy Week. This consoled me and I regained my peace.

82. **3-26-97**
Graces Available for the Asking

During the Rosary with Father, I saw a stream of light shining from the heavens to earth and illuminating a calendar from Holy Thursday to the octave of Easter, Divine Mercy Sunday. Our Lady said: *Child, these are graces for the asking. Let my children who have the grace to pray ask for those who do not pray. Ask for the graces of conversion for all souls. An abundance of Divine Light will stream from heaven to earth in these graced holy days.*

My little children turn toward the heavens and seek God! I implore you to rise above the world and its lowly spirit. I implore you to consider your soul; to look to God for all that you need. All the devils in hell have been released on your generation, but God offers each one the grace to overcome the devil; to battle the spirit of the world.

In these holiest of days dedicated to Jesus, pray unceasingly, offer everything to God and call down His Mercy from the heavens to the earth. I pray for you. Persevere, dear little children. My Son died and rose for you, that you may live forever. By His stripes you are healed! Believe and hope. Trust! Pray for those who do not pray because they suffer from lack of communication with God. I love you. Your Mother

After the Rosary, when praying over Father, I saw his soul as an enclosed garden but the gate was wide open. Our Lady said: *Before his conversion , he left the gate open, allowing many things to come and go according to his will. But now he has surrendered! As Mother, I stand guard together with the many angels, to open and close the gate according to God's Will. He persevered for God and belongs entirely to the Father, Son, and Holy Spirit. My heart rejoices to surround and protect this priest-son.*

83. **3-26-97 (B)**
A Storm of Temptations!

I am bombarded with evil temptations; weary from the battle which is fierce and continuous. The enemy hounds me constantly. I fear I am backsliding rapidly; sinking like in quicksand. I am tormented by the devil with every kind of lie.

"O my God, steady my soul! My little ship is traveling in a terrible storm besieged in every way. I fear I will sink. This very night I entertained the temptations, which assailed me constantly. What sorrow! Have pity on me Lord! Steady my soul! By grace alone will I live and overcome this torment of the spirit! Grant me fortitude! Mary, my Mother, help me to persevere and fight against all temptations. And please help me to surrender to all that God permits to happen to me and my family. Amen."

84. **3-27-97**
Tell Me: Why Do You Love Me?

It is Holy Thursday. I went to church for the "Washing of the Feet." Following the service I remained in adoration of the Blessed Sacrament where I was bombarded with temptations regarding the failures and faults of myself and family. The devil amplified every problem and I was overcome with intense discouragement and angry at myself and the family. Suddenly, Jesus said: ***Soul, are you here to adore Me?** I replied: "Yes, Lord." He continued: ***Soul, then tell Me, why do you love Me?**

Jesus, I love you because you are worthy of all my love. You are utterly, indescribably loveable! I love your Beauty, Goodness, and Majesty. You are faithful, steadfast, my rock and salvation. You are the lover of my soul and of all souls. You are the Love that sustains all of creation: the Lamb who takes away my sin and that of the world. You are Mercy; forgetful of my wickedness, transfiguring wretchedness into your own Beauty. I love Your Presence in my soul; the way You bring me to Life.

You are God but you humble Yourself to come to me. I love Your gentleness and strength. It is Your delight to give to creatures and You do so unceasingly and generously. Every moment, from the beginning to the end, is charged with Your Divine Love. You are the Light and I love Your radiance. I love You because You are Truth and in You there is no falsehood. O how I love the Truth that You are! And I love Your Justice, correcting the unjust and delivering the innocent.

O Jesus, You are my Savior, my Redeemer, full of dignity. Yet You empty Yourself out like a slave for souls whether they love You or do not love You. O God, who can fathom Your magnificence, Your omnipotence? Your Power is incomprehensible. And Your pure Love overcomes every evil. O Word Incarnate, You took on human lowliness becoming the full revelation of God for all ages. Your breath creates goodness. O Jesus, I love everything about You – in my own poor way. And I beg you to grant me the grace to love You more each day of my life.

O Jesus, on this Holy Thursday, we remember the Last Supper, the institution of the Eucharist, Your Body with us until the end of time. You are the souls sustenance. We remember how You bent to wash the apostles' feet. O humble Lamb of God! Praise be to You for every good! I love how You cover my nakedness; how You illumine my way with Light. O Jesus, what a wonder You are! Name above all names, be adored eternally! When I call on You, You are there! Always and everywhere, You hear my cry. You lavish my soul with Divine Love and cause me to long all the more for You. I have an unquenchable thirst. The more I drink of Your Love, the greater the thirst. O Jesus, You are my Beloved and I am Yours.

Thank You, my God, for teaching me by Your Own Hand and causing my poor soul to love You to its little capacity, yet to the

full. Keep me in You, Lord. It is a mystery! You are more tangible
to me than any human being that I can see or touch. I do not see
You with my eyes or touch You with my hands, but I know You
more deeply than I know anyone else and I love You passionately.
It is a mystery! Be glorified!

85. **3-28-97** Good Friday
Living Water: New Life

In the Rosary with Father, I received an image of a human heart
which was as dry as a desert floor, full of cracks from no water.
Then I saw the pierced Heart of Jesus on Calvary with the water
and the blood gushing out from Him on the Cross. It fell upon the
dry human heart. Suddenly the image of the heart changed to a
globe of the world which was as parched as the heart. As I gazed at
it, I could see that at its deepest core, there was a wellspring, underground, where the water would spring forth to irrigate the parched
soil. I saw new life spring up. What appeared to be dead was brought
back to life. The graces of Good Friday will flow eternally.

86. **3-31-97**
A Lesson

Following Mass and Holy Hour, a terrible storm assailed my
soul. Evil spirits of rebellion, futility, discouragement, anger, re-
sentment, overwhelmed me and I did not pray to fight them off this
time. I somehow just let them assail me, I would not rebuke them.
The most terrible temptations were against faith and hope. I was
somehow being convinced that I have been deceived in the spiritual realm and that the spiritual life is an illusion and began to
reject the spiritual reality. I became increasingly knotted up inside
of myself. Rebellion seemed to overtake me. I would not open my
mouth to speak because at some level I was aware that nothing
good would come out of me at this time. I remained locked up
inside of myself with the evil spirits playing around in my mind,
entertaining the lies that were being presented about the spiritual

reality. I spent most of the day in this terrible state, refusing to turn to God with this. It was an agony!

In the evening, a potentially dangerous incident happened to my family, but God protected my son. Just when I was convinced that God abandoned me, He saved my son from harm. Realizing that this was a big grace, I turned in gratitude to the Lord. As soon as I did so, the evil temptations lifted completely. I was foolish to be so stubborn as to refuse prayer and entertain the temptations. It has been a big lesson!

87. **4-1-97**
The Eucharist Integrates

At Holy Communion, I said, "My God, you are with me now. Inside of me is Your Body, Blood, Soul, and Divinity. Know that I am sorry for my behavior yesterday and that I love You with all my heart."

Immediately, I received an image of my being in a disintegrated state, my body seemingly dismembered: the heart torn into pieces and the spirit going in a different direction. Then I saw my soul and in the deepest center was Jesus, His Body, Blood, Soul, and Divinity, the Host I had just received.

I observed that His Presence, the Host inside of me, was like a magnet that pulled together – integrated, my body, heart, mind, and spirit. He makes me whole and well. He is the glue that keeps me together. There is harmony within me because of His gift, the Eucharist.

"O holiest of Sacraments, thank you for the gift of Yourself. Holy Presence with me, hold me together in Your Love forever. My Lord and Savior, I love you boundlessly!"

88. **4-4-97** Prayer Group
Growing Pains

My dear children, I am your Mother of mercy. I am with you again to bless and teach you. Thank you, my dearly beloved ones, for permitting me to assist you along the way. You are a most precious family of souls in the eyes of the Most Holy Trinity. Know that you have received an abundance of heavenly grace along the way to form you to give honor and glory to God.

I observe that you are undergoing growing pains. This is part of the growth process. It will strengthen and unite you. The enemy targets you with a spirit of confusion, fear and division. In order to proceed in the way of the Divine Will, you must be of one spirit and one heart. Pray and uphold one another. Increase your trust and confidence in the Holy Spirit who is working in each one of you in a very special way. It is He who works over the soil of your heart. You are being tried and tested for the sake of your sanctity. Do not doubt. Each one of you has the same Holy Spirit. But each has a different gift of the Spirit. Persevere in prayer. God's work will proceed and be accomplished. Do not worry but trust! Have you not been led each step of the way by the Holy Spirit who called you each by name to form this prayer family? What is built by God is not torn down. There will be unity based on Love. You will falter if you walk alone, but together you will not falter.

You who have received God's abundant mercy are called now to be servants of mercy for other souls. Lead souls to drink of the fountain of Divine Mercy. Assist souls to learn of forgiveness and reconciliation. Many souls will be healed through your efforts and prayerful intercession. The mercy you give will come back to you a hundredfold. God is never outdone in generosity.

I bless you in the name of the Most Holy Trinity. This is a most holy season (Easter) and many graces are available for the asking. Ask for yourself and for other souls. Graces are flowing from the pierced Heart of my Son, Jesus, to enliven faith, hope, and love. Many never avail themselves of the graces that are offered.

Thank you for being my little, little ones. God is good and worthy of all your love and trust. He blesses His creation. He never forsakes souls but seeks out the most lost, sick, weak, troubled and forgotten souls. He is the Savior of all sinners. Allow Him to use you as He pleases. And when He puts you in a period of waiting, in silence and darkness, rest in His Heart of Love. Wait on Him. Your patience will be rewarded. Do not be afraid but trust. The hand of Almighty God is upon you. Do not strive to know where He is lead-

ing you. Strive to live His Will every step of the way. Follow Him one step at a time, taking in the fullness of each moment with Him and in Him. He will finish what He begins. Pray and you will have peace in His Love. I love you. Your Mother

89. **4-6-97**
Divine Mercy

While working at a conference celebrating the Feast of Divine Mercy, I received an image of the entire area transfigured into an ocean of God's Mercy. Each person was immersed in the Precious Blood. Then each soul became a little ship, filled with the most precious cargo of God's Mercy becoming the vessels, which would carry His Mercy out into the world. We formed the little ships that form the armada of God's Divine Mercy for souls.

In retaliation for working to spread the message of Divine Mercy, I was severely attacked by the devil. After a day of abundant graces for all, suddenly at the Mass, I was besieged by spirits of aversion to God's people and the Church. The devil portrayed the people in a most negative light. The aversion to working in the Church increased and there were terrible thoughts of negativity and suspicion, even regarding the priests saying the Mass! I became hypersensitive and hypercritical to everything and it all seemed imperfect. I was overcome with agitation, critical of everything. This was so powerful that I was tempted to flee the assembly. I could not regain my peace. Agitation escalated and futility increased until I was thinking that I could no longer work in the Church. I should quit!

In the midst of tremendous healing graces, which were being poured out upon the assembly, I was struggling with these temptations. It amazes me how the devil can attack to block out all the good in my midst and emphasize the negative. I was extra vulnerable to attacks because of physical fatigue. And my own pride was involved as well; the desire that everything be perfect opens the door for attacks.

After this severe attack, there was rebellion inside of me. I wanted all suffering; physical, emotional, spiritual, to stop. Everything in me was crying out, enough! I went to my spiritual director and told him everything. He heard my confession and prayed over me. It took him three times to expel the evil spirits present to my soul. Then peace came.

As I fell asleep Jesus said: **Your suffering gained grace for the assembly. I poured out My merciful healing graces to others. Let that be your consolation. You are My pupil and I am teaching you. Grow for Me. The attacks upon your soul, which I allow, cause you to know the enemy, yourself, and Me. You must learn, My child. Peace be with you. Rest in Me. I love you and will never abandon you. Your Jesus**

90. 4-7-97
Let It Be Done According to Your Word

During the Rosary with Father, at the Nativity decade, I saw the birth scene at Bethlehem. Suddenly Our Lady said: *My fiat at the Annunciation facilitated the birth of my Son, Jesus. My yes to God's Divine Will brought forth the fruit of my womb and gave birth to Life through my Son, Jesus. When you respond with your own fiat to God, when you say, "Let it be done unto me according to Your Word," you dispose yourself for the birthing of new life in your own soul.*

Dear children, entrust yourselves to the Holy Spirit because He is the One who empowers your soul to utter those most precious words "Fiat. Yes, Lord." The Holy Spirit will guide you to a consistent attitude of yes. This is the disposition of docility. The more docile you are, the more teachable you are. The Holy Spirit is your Divine Teacher, but He can only teach those who want to be taught. Only the little ones desire to be led by the Spirit. You must be little to receive Wisdom. Humility disposes you because humility is Truth.

I am with you, little children, to assist you to say yes to God, to say yes to His Divine and Perfect Will for yourselves, your families and the world. You cannot respond with your own fiat if you are not listening to Him in prayer. When you take the time to listen to God, He speaks in the quiet of your heart and His voice is heard and understood in your heart. But your heart must be pure, free of any idols.

Little ones, some of you give to God an initial "yes" and this continues for awhile. But many fail to continue living in a constant attitude of yes to God. Often, when commitment or suffering is asked, the yes that you gave initially is changed to "no, Lord." It is only in and through the Person of the Holy Spirit that you can live in a consistent attitude of yes to God. Therefore, always invoke the Holy Spirit and ask for the grace to respond, "Let it be done to me according to Your Word." Let the desires of your heart conform to the Will of God. This is the hallmark of a true disciple and child of God. Be led, little children, to closer union with our Triune God, then will you possess joy and peace and you will have Love. Thank you for allowing my Immaculate Heart to embrace you. I love you. Your Mother

91. **4-7-97 (B)**
The Child Jesus Pleads to the Father

During the Rosary with Father, I saw Jesus as a young boy, perhaps seven years old. He held the globe of the earth in His Hand as He stood before the throne of the Father in heaven. There was a long, loving gaze between the Father and the Son, then both turned their eyes to the globe. The child, Jesus, spoke to the Father with utmost reverence saying: **Father, You so loved the world that You sent Me to it as a child, that I might teach every man to be a child of Yours. Father, the time is at hand, is it not? Let this be the hour of transfiguration of the world. Father, touch Your creation with Your Paternal Grace and cause them to become little children. Cause them to give You Honor and Glory. Father, Your Will be done on earth as it is in heaven. My Heart, one with the Immaculate Heart, gathers little ones unto You. Humble mankind now. Cause them to come to Life. Allow them to turn to You, Father. I died and I live that all may enter into Your Kingdom. Let it be done. Amen and amen.**

92. **4-7-97 (C)**
Learn to Trust in Me

Today Father told me that, in prayer, on 4-5-97, Jesus gave him a message of encouragement for me and I was filled with gratitude saying, "Lord, who am I that You would grant me a priest who can bathe my poor soul in Your Own Divine Love?"

Jesus said: **You are nothing, *Soul, but I grant grace to whom I please. I am Love and it is My Divine Will to lavish your poor soul with Love. My priest is full of charity. This sanctifies him and upholds your soul in its time of purification. I am taking you to the heights of My Own suffering that you might glorify the Father, and save souls with Me. You are protected in the shelter of the Wing of the Holy Spirit. Receive My blessings through My priest as I will it. I bless you both. He is My beloved priest, whose heart is pure and teachable, growing daily in docility, wisdom, and love.**

*Soul, I love you with a Perfect Love beyond your comprehension. Allow Me to be your Love and Master. Bless Me, the Lord, your God, with your obedience. Will you humble yourself for Me?

I replied: "Jesus, do You not humble Yourself for me? On the Cross, in the Eucharist, and in all the graces, do You not humble Yourself for me? Yes, Lord, I will strive to imitate your own humility because I love You and want to please You. Grant me the grace to do this, Lord."

*Soul your response pleases Me. You and Father must grow in trust of Me. Know that My Heart is tender and merciful and it is the refuge of souls. Your suffering increases when you lack trust. Each attack of the devil is permitted that you grow in trust of Me.

Eventually, you will not lose your peace so easily. You are proceeding toward this; learning to recognize the enemy, know yourself and trust in Me. I am teaching you because I love you infinitely and want to teach others through you. Trust! Know that your love covers a multitude of sin and be at peace in Me. Have joy! I am your Jesus

93. **4-8-97**
St. Therese Helps

I awake in a state of extreme sorrow. It seems that I am misery itself! I struggle with temptations of despair, futility, and extreme sadness. It seems that the weight of the sins of the world presses upon me and crushes me. I cannot pray and missed Mass.

Throughout the day this attack continued, but I began to pray by repeatedly saying the Holy Name of Jesus. I am in a terrible state of sorrow that practically paralyzes me from functioning. Though my family seems to add to the sorrow today, I must pull myself together to take care of them. This was difficult because I couldn't seem to grasp onto enough love.

For some reason, I could not focus on the Father, Jesus, the Holy Spirit or Mother Mary. But I was drawn to a book on St. Therese of Lisieux and wholeheartedly I said, "Therese! Hurry and help me, please!" I opened a large picture book to an 8 x 10 picture of her beautiful serene face, and I read these words on the opposite page of her picture. Suddenly, I understood the lesson that God was giving to me through this Saint and peace and joy overcame me.

Three weeks before Therese entered Carmel, she confided her desires to her sister writing, "Pauline, when Jesus places me on the blessed shore of Carmel, I want to give myself entirely to Him. I want to live for Him. Oh no, I will not fear His blows, for even in the most bitter sufferings, one always feels that it is His gentle Hand that strikes. I felt it strongly in Rome at the very moment when I would have thought the earth could give way under my steps.

"Once I am in Carmel I will desire only one thing: always to suffer with Jesus. Life passes so quickly that it would truly be better to have a very beautiful crown along with a little suffering than to have an ordinary one without any sufferings. And I think that suffering borne joyfully helps one love God better for all eternity. Why, by suffering, you can even save souls. Ah! Pauline, if at the moment of my death, I could bring one soul to Jesus, how happy I would be! There would be a soul snatched from the fires of hell to praise God for all eternity!"

Title: *Therese and Lisieux* by Helmuth Nills Loose and Pierre Discouvement. Wm. B. Eeerdmans Publishing Co., Grand Rapids, MI 49503-1996, pg. 94.

94. **4-11-97** Prayer Group
Do You Love Me?

I received an image of the Sacred Heart of Jesus, pierced. Blood and water gushed from His pierced Heart onto us. Jesus spoke: **My dear children, I, your Jesus, bless you and am with you to teach My Holy Way. My dear ones, if you are not growing, you are going backward. Growth has nothing to do with what you are feeling. Growth takes place in the darkness of faith. I seek growth in obedience, silence, humility, and commitment. Adorn yourselves with all the virtues of the Immaculate Heart of Mary, our Mother, because her Heart and Mine are One Heart that cannot be separated. Grow in union with Me!**

I am your Redeemer. I laid down My Life for your sin and the sin of the whole world. Do you resemble Me in My Passion? You are called to be My reflection, My echo. Grow in love! Fall in love with Me because I am in love with you! You are full of imperfection and utterly needy but I love you with My tender, merciful Heart. Seek My Face. Seek My Voice.

Come before Me in prayer. Allow Me to ask you, "Why do you love Me?" Let Me hear from your heart. Why do you love the Lord, your God? Then listen in silence so that I can tell you, "I love you." Unworthy as you are, you are most precious in My sight. I long to use you toward the redemption of souls. But I cannot if you do not offer your "yes." I await your continuous surrender. Please allow Me freedom in your soul. Trust Me.

Do not turn to people to find the perfect love that you require. You will find perfect love in Me, alone. There is too much talk and discussion instead of prayer. Bring everything to Me. Accept My Counsel, My Holy Spirit. Meet Me in silence and solitude. There you will find the answer. If you find silence and darkness, praise My Holy Name, because I am in the silence

and darkness. Be faithful to prayer and wait on Me because My timing is perfect toward bringing the greatest Good out of every situation, for every soul.

You must grow now, My dear ones, in every way. I will test your fidelity and your love! How much do you love Me? How much faith do you have when you are surrounded by suffering? Show Me and I will bless your every effort. Nothing goes unnoticed by your Lord, your God. There are not secrets with Me. Every movement of your heart, I see. Every thought that crosses your mind, I know. Look to Me and I will reveal My Heart and My Love to you. I do not withhold Myself from you.

You form part of the army of soldiers preparing the way for the era of peace. You must be fit for battle. Your only weapon is Love. But there is nothing more powerful than Love! To love is a self-sacrifice and I call you to Love because it glorifies the Father and beautifies you. Therefore, grow in Love every day! This can only happen through grace. I give this grace in prayer and through the Sacraments. Look at Me, not yourself! If you pray, you will grow! Come. My Heart is wide open. It is pierced for love of you. Drink of the fountain of My Love and Mercy. Allow Me to love you. Love Me in return as I love you.

In the name of the Most Holy Trinity, I bless you in this Holy Season (Easter). Be at peace in My Love. Your Jesus

95. 4-13-97
A Test of Love

There is suffering, which I believe has come from God's Hand, in which I feel cut off from love. At prayer group, I received an image of a padlock being put on my heart.

While I have been tried in faith and hope, love has always been abundant, so strong that it held everything together for me. In this test, I have no sense of being loved. It is as if I have been cut off from either being loved or loving. I struggle to describe this but it is an intense reality in my soul; an anguish of the heart. It seems to be a torture of the spirit when I can see and know that love is all around me but seemingly, it is not for me. It is present, but I cannot touch it or be touched by it. I reach for it, long for it, but it always escapes me. It is ever present but beyond me.

In addition to this trial, a certain soul is able to heap terrible mental anguish upon me; used daily to attack me in various ways. And I must remain silent, without any retaliation, because this is what God is asking from me. My only consolation is in knowing that I am doing God's Will and this has been discerned with Father and the prayer community who help me through this trying time.

It would not be an exaggeration to say that at every moment there is suffering of my heart. If I try to distract myself from it, it doesn't help. If I try to compensate for it, it doesn't stop but makes it worse. There is nothing for me to do but accept it and trust that God will use it and bring good from it.

I realize in suffering this that I am among many of the faithful members of the Body of Christ who suffer in the same manner. Persecution of God's disciples and a lack of love is rampant in the world today. In allowing me to suffer this, I am united to the Lord in Gethsemane and at Calvary. Together with Him I cry out, "Father, let this cup pass from Me" and "Father, has Thou forsaken me?" My response can only be the same as the Lord's: "Yet not mine but Your Will be done" and "Father, forgive them for they know not what they do. Into Your Hands, I commend my spirit."

96. **4-14-97**
Love Tested Again

In church following Mass and Holy Hour, a prayer group member came to me and shared an image received, in which I was seen with the crown of thorns on my head, covered in blood, hair matted down with it and dripping onto my face, which appeared in agony. And the words were heard, "She would gladly trade this kind of suffering for the terrible mental anguish which she is made to endure for so long now." After sharing this, he left and I remained alone in prayer.

I asked Jesus, "Will it end soon?" He replied: **It is not yet time, *Soul. Be patient. You are suffering for the sake of the** conversion of many souls. You are another victim lamb. Will you continue?

Weeping profusely and full of pain I replied, "Yes, Jesus. I will continue."

*Soul, I alone know the mental torture that you endure. I observe the mutilation of your human heart. Your suffering is immense and I know it. Greater than your suffering is the Good that I will bring out of it. Because your mind is anguished and heart mutilated, I give to you My Own Mind, My Own Heart. Yes, you resemble Me in My Passion – so that you can resemble Me in My Glory. In your hour of desolation, you are not alone, My bride. Yet I allow you to perceive only loneliness and abandonment. We are One and nothing can separate us.

"Jesus, must You try me in the area of love now? It is most difficult."

*Soul, I am teaching you. The whole world is turning away from Love and I will that you know how My creation suffers from the absence of True Love, that in turn you will pray and help them! I am teaching you the desolation of My creation due to sin and the lies of the enemy. Learn this so that you can help to overcome it. That is why you are asked to lay down your life for others. Many will live because of your sacrifice. You are with Me and in Me, therefore, Love is not abandoning you, only testing and teaching you. I am sharing My Heart with you. My Love upholds you. You would have collapsed by now if I did not uphold you. Grow for Me. I love you and I am yours. Jesus

97. **4-15-97**
Fear Not!

At Holy Communion I received an image of myself walking along a flat pathway. I was surefooted, walking at a steady pace because the pathway was flat and clear for as long as I could see. Quite suddenly, a mountain appeared on the pathway right before me. I halted, stood at the base and looked straight up to the top.

Jesus said: **Beloved, fear not! Whatever obstacles are put in your path, I shall overcome for you. Observe how I can carry**

you over that mountain in an instant. (I received an image of Jesus doing just that.) **The pathway represents the way of the Divine Will. It is the path that Divine Providence has set before you to walk. There is only one thing which can block that path for you and it is your own human will opposed to the Divine Will. You are free to choose.**

Please write for My people.

Beloved ones, I, your Jesus, have overcome every obstacle to your salvation. Remember this! Do not be afraid when obstacles appear in your path. Satan will place stumbling blocks as you strive to walk faithfully in the ways of Love, striving to be holy.

I have gone before you to show you precisely how to obey the Father. I learned obedience by what I suffered. You have been baptized into My death so that you can rise to My Glory. Whatever you are made to suffer now, in these days of great confusion and evil, will serve to form your crown of glory.

There will come a time when it will seem that evil has won but accept no lie! I am the Victor and victory is yours in Me. All that belongs to the Father, Son, and Holy Spirit is for your Good. We will not forsake you!

I have bent from heaven to earth to come to you to fore-warn you of these times of darkness. Indeed, the heavens have opened up and showered you with grace, covering you like dew. It is there for the asking. Those who have eyes that are open, see it. Many are indeed prepared for battle. Yet more are not prepared. Even on earth is there not an army of men that defend the rest? My Mother has prepared such an army. I have said My Glory shall be made manifest on earth and I shall transfigure all of creation into My Beauty. And is not My Beauty – Love? Where Love abounds, evil is cast out! Where Love abounds, there is no fear!

Before My apostles, Peter, James, and John, were made to observe My Passion, I fortified their faith and hope in Me by revealing My Glory at Mount Tabor. (The Transfiguration.) **I am doing this for you, My apostles of the latter days, through the special graces, signs and wonders of the present time. Indeed, the days of My Passion shall repeat and yet every disciple of Mine will know that Life is victorious over death!**

Any who come to Me shall not be rejected. Whoever acknowledges his sin shall be welcomed to My Mercy. Let there be no obstacles to your faith; no stumbling block to your hope; no suffering that impedes your Love. I am with you always and everywhere. Have courage! Your Jesus

98. **4-16-97**
Blows to the Church

When praying the Rosary with Father, I received an image of a sledgehammer hitting the Church (represented by St. Peter's Basilica). There was a powerful and sudden blow to the Church and a gaping hole appeared in the structure of it. I was overcome with an intense burden in my heart for the Church.

Jesus said: **Beloved ones, let it be known that My Church, My Mystical Body, will be dealt many blows from within and without! Do not be scandalized but count on her foundation to be indestructible! All of hell unleashed upon her shall not prevail against her! My Church will live out these days in militant battle with the forces of evil. She will bear many battle scars and appear beaten down. But she will overcome all that is against her and emerge in victory, a reflection of My own Glory!**

My sorrow increases as I observe My House become divided. The Holy Spirit does not divide, but unifies. But the Holy Spirit is Truth and Truth does not stand with untruth. My sorrow is for the tender, innocent hearts of the faithful who will suffer confusion and discouragement in observing the polarization of the Mystical Body. Faith, hope, and love will be lacking and everyone shall be tested. I, Myself, shall be the Good Shepherd. I will shepherd the faithful flock and together we will cry out in prayer for unbelievers and pawns of the enemy.

The Father will hear the cry of His people and pour His Grace upon earth to unify the Body and restore creation to Love. The Communion of Saints will extend from heaven to earth where My Holy Name will be worshipped and adored. Until that appointed time, there will be much to suffer toward restoration. If your lamp is full of oil, let it burn brightly now

and provide the light for those in need or darkness. **My Heart of Love embraces each person and I do not desire to lose even one whom the Father has given to Me. Pray with Me and keep watch with Me. I love you. Jesus**

99. **4-18-97**
Never Degrade Yourself

After confession, I went before the tabernacle to pray my penance. Immediately Jesus spoke as I knelt before Him in the Blessed Sacrament.

***Soul, My beloved. Do you not realize that you are a temple of the Holy Spirit?** Here, I saw Jesus hanging on the cross, alive and bleeding over me. From here He continued. **I have already borne the insults and injury that comes upon you. Do not inflict further degradation upon yourself. You belong to Me and are most precious in My sight! Please do not harm My Temple of the Holy Spirit! Do not defile the flower that you are. Do you not know that your fragrance rises to Me as holy and pure? Do you not realize that I love you? Never degrade what I love! Peace and Mercy. Your Jesus**

100. **4-20-97**
The Pontificate of Pope John Paul II

At home in the beginning of the Rosary with Father, I saw St. Peter's Basilica in Rome and Vatican City. My sight was drawn to the window of the Pope's room from which he can see the piazza. The Holy Father appeared to be a in a state of deep contemplation as he looked out of his window. It was as if he was reviewing all of Church history. It seemed that the Church's past was being shown to him, playing out its drama before his mind's eye as if a movie was unfolding before him.

While his mind's eye was reviewing the history of the Church in every detail, his heart was one with everything that he saw. It seemed to me that the entire history of the Church was woven into the very fabric of his heart. Words cannot express the "union" that I was given to see between the Church and this Pope. I somehow understood at a deeper level the depth of love that this Pope has for the Mystical Body of Christ and his union with it; past, present and future!

Once the entire history of the Church had been reviewed, he went back to take a closer look at St. Peter. There seemed to take place a fusion of his spirit with Peter's. I sensed the Holy Father's profound humility in the presence of St. Peter coupled with a sense of awe and appreciation. Peter shed his blood for the Church. John Paul seemed deeply inspired by St. Peter's love of the Lord and the sacrifice of laying down one's life for the Church.

In this grace, my heart is inflamed with love for John Paul; the person, his dignity, his unselfish love; also for the office of Christ's Vicar, his authority from God, and I have deeper love for Holy Mother Church. Imperfect as she is, her maternal milk has nourished the world throughout the ages.

In the image of Pope John Paul reviewing the Church's history, I sensed that he was pondering every detail of her existence as "Church militant", her battle against the spirit of the world, her fight against evil. I sensed he was loving her for all the "good" that comes to the world through her. And it seemed he was tenderly forgiving her past errors. Throughout this grace, as I observed it, I sensed that the Pope was looking at the past and the present, always with an eye toward the future. The Pope's interior disposition seemed filled with joy, hope, and love. I sensed that this stemmed from his awareness of a new springtime for the Church, a time for her to enter into her glory. It seemed that he understood that his pontificate, his ministry, would form the gateway into the springtime of the Church and civilization of love.

His heart is already there. He suffers extreme longing for it for the sake of every person. I understood there is no concern about a personal cost to him. He lays down his life for love of God and love of every person. He is another Peter. He is the Pope of the glorified Church, the shepherd directing the faithful flock into the era of holiness. His sacrifice is supreme, but his love is greater.

Then the scene changed to an interior view of what appeared to be the Pope's private bedroom. John Paul, dressed in white robes, lay on his bed, in a state of rest. My heart was filled with joy and peace, but I was not given understanding.

After receiving this, I entered into a prayer state. At the closing prayers by Father, I came out of this state and saw again the same image of the Pope, as if to imprint it deeper into my heart.

101. **4-21-97**
Terrible Temptations!

Journal: The lies of the enemy that bombard my soul consist of these:
1) Isolate yourself. Jesus and me alone! No one else! Forget community.
2) I am a fool to pray and ask Jesus about everything. I can use my own brain to make my own decisions.
3) No need to do His Will in every situation; day in and day out. My human will is all right sometimes. Do as I please.
4) I am worthless and my life counts for nothing. It is futile to follow the Lord. It brings nothing but sorrow. Others are enlightened to this and I just do not get it.
5) I am justified in being angry and I should retaliate and defend myself. It is alright to be angry inside.
6) Have fun. Everyone else is having a good time in life except me. Sacrifice does not pay.
7) Be bold! Quiet endurance is useless and foolish. Speak out! Break the silence!
8) Lighten up! Have some drinks and have a good time. Life is passing me by.
9) Get away. Run away – perhaps, Vegas?
10) Blame my spiritual director, he insists that I follow the way of Jesus! Let him be the holy one. He's a priest. I'm just a lay person!
11) Get some new friends. Drop the prayer group. Break away form them and the spiritual life.
12) Give up the battle. The devil is going to win in the end.
    I rebuke all of these temptations but I am hounded! I do not give in by the grace of God.

102. **4-22-97**
Rebellion

After Mass and Holy Hour, I said to the Lord, "Jesus, this suffering is overwhelming! Everything is misery to me! I was going to go on when suddenly, Jesus said: ***Soul! You are like a little donkey kicking up its heels in rebellion! You are learning obedience and it is painful to you because your human will is very strong! You must learn obedience of faith in order to go where I intend to take you! In the future, this lesson will prove most beneficial to your soul. Forsake your desires for My holy and Divine Will and draw grace for yourself and others. I love you. Jesus**

103. **4-22-97 (B)**
In the Rosary, Through the Life of Christ

During the Rosary with Father I received the following:

1) At the decade of the Agony in the Garden I received an image of Jesus bent over the rock in Gethsemane, in agony, sweating blood. Then the entire universe seemed to be present, contained in that garden of agony. The rock upon which Jesus was bent transfigured into the Church. His agony continued as He prayed for all of creation. His Precious Blood covered the rock, the Church. Then came an illumination wherein I understood more deeply that the Church is for every man, not just her members. I saw her as the Mother through whom souls receive nourishment. The members are doubly blessed to receive the sacramental graces, but her graces extend out to every nation and people. And the Holy Sacrifice of the Mass in which her members are truly blessed, also benefits the whole world. Good comes upon creation through the offering of each sacrifice of the Mass.

2) At the decade of the Scourging at the Pillar, I saw Christians throughout the world being scourged. Some were lightly

scourged and others, severely. However, there wasn't a Christian who escaped some form of scourging from the world. As each one suffered some type of persecution, Jesus was with us. I saw that Jesus and the Christians transfigured one another. The Lord suffers and never leaves us. Yet we will be stretched for the sake of Love, for upholding His Holy Name.

3) At The Crowning of Thorns decade, I saw the globe with a crown of thorns surrounding it. On top of the crown of thorns I saw the magnificent Dove of the Holy Spirit. Rays of grace passed from the Holy Spirit through the Crown of Thorns, which bled upon the earth and penetrated the parched soil, enriching it.

4) At the decade of the "Carrying of the Heavy Cross", I saw Christians around the world, carrying very heavy crosses and proceeding along the Via Dolorosa to Calvary. Suddenly, Our Lady became present to each one and helped us carry the cross. She was for us, a Simon of Cyrene. And I saw the holy women, Veronica, Mary Magdalene, and others, step forward to assist in the carrying of the crosses. Then the Communion of Saints stepped forward to help also. The scene changed to include the non-Christians carrying very heavy crosses. The Christians, whom they had persecuted, stepped up to help them. Love began to unify.

5) At the decade of Jesus Dying on the Cross, I saw a soul who had broken a covenant and betrayed God. He walked the earth in heavy shackles. Suddenly, Jesus said: **Soul, pride forms the shackles. In a quest for freedom, he is bound all the more by pride. No soul is self-sufficient, but pride deceives a soul to believe that it can be self-sufficient. Pray very much for this soul. He is in grave danger.** Then I saw a judge's gavel ready to strike the wood, and I understood how critical it was for me to pray for this soul. God caused me to ask for mercy rather than justice. Then Jesus said: ***Soul, love covers a multitude of sin. Be at peace. How quickly you lose your peace because you do not trust Me. My beloved bride, I suffer with you and My Grace causes you to endure and persevere. You are learning the meaning of the words, "Wait**

upon the Lord." Blessed are you who wait upon Me. Continue to be obedient to My Divine Will. Suffer silently in Me, with Me. Do not block the Love that I give to you because you are consumed with the pain. I am loving you always that you may love as I love. You are full of imperfection but through this trial, Love is perfecting you. Again I say to you, Love is above all else. You are My beloved bride. Drink My Blood and live in Me. Your will is being crucified and this is for the good. I offer you something much more perfect – My Own Divine Will. The perfection that you seek is found only in Me. Be patient with yourself and family. Your soul is very poor on its own, but I have enriched you with Myself, My Presence in you. I will use you to enrich many others. I must reign in you completely and in you there can be no rivals. I love you. Jesus

104. **4-25-97**
Priest's Prayers

At a prayer meeting, some priests prayed over me. The Lord told one priest to remind me that He is faithful to His promises but it may be only after the fact that I will know this. Then he received and image of evil spirits trying to harass and agitate me.

My spiritual director received an image of me being placed in a large desert; a place of battle, prayer, silence and solitude; like Jesus before public ministry.

105. **4-27-97**
Jesus Warns of Persecution of Christians

At home I prayed "Jesus, You have upheld my soul in abundant grace for two days. Thank you, Lord. Your Presence is constant and brings me deep peace, silence and confidence. How glorious are your visitations to a soul! For two days, your Divine Love pierces my heart almost constantly to remind me that Love loves me, Love is with me, in me, and seeking my love in return.

Your Divine Touch is like the surgeon's scalpel. Ever so gently You score the tissue of my heart causing it to bleed, so that it remains open instead of closing up within itself. In the midst of persecution, your Divine Love operates on my heart that it functions as the life-giving organ of love.

O my Jesus, how often I have doubted the One so worthy of all my trust! Forgive me, Jesus, for thinking that I can take care of myself when You are the perfect caretaker of my soul. Surrendering to You is easy one moment and difficult the next. How strong is my own human will that resists constant surrender. My God, take away my resistance. How patient You are with my poor soul."

Jesus said: *Soul of My Cross, Love is with you. Please write My words.

My lamb, you have lowered your voice to hear Mine. Treat Me as your King. Allow Me to reign in you. Become My Kingdom. Love thirsts for love. Love thirsts for souls. My bride, serve your King, your Groom, by serving souls. Cause souls to come to Me. Your heart is pierced as Mine is pierced for love of souls.

*Soul of My Cross, listen and let My words penetrate you. The darkest hour of man is close at hand. You cannot fathom the evil that has penetrated the heart of mankind. But I say to you, there is an undercurrent of evil forces that work feverishly at this hour, remaining hidden so as not to be discovered until all is set in place to perpetuate the greatest of evils, the murder of faith, hope, and love.

There will be much to suffer in the days to come. Evil will rear its destructive head and deal deadly blows to every nation, church, and people. It will happen suddenly although it is already underway, but in a hidden fashion. The Holy Spirit has come to the four corners of the earth to alert souls, to awaken from slumber, to prepare for great persecution.

The enemy plots to crush faith, to eradicate hope, and erase love. The dragon will attempt to erect a new god, an evil one. And men, without roots in faith, hope, and love, will look to this new god and serve him because he will tickle their ears and bribe their hearts.

I, the Lamb who takes away the sin of the world, the One worthy to open the seal, the One with the keys to the netherworld, will allow My creation to be tried for a period of time. All the while, My sheep will hear My Voice. For I am the Good Shepherd and My Sheep know Me and I know those who follow My Voice. In the time of trial, My Own will be tested and purified, remaining always with the One True Shepherd.

For those who do not know My Voice, who do not know The Good Shepherd, there will be great difficulty because they are easily swept away. That is why these days of preparation are so necessary to strengthen faith, hope, and love. Heaven has bent to earth to prepare the world for its greatest battle. The floodgates of grace have been opened for this generation so as to prepare mankind for the coming trials and persecution. There is a remnant battling for souls who have not yet availed themselves of My Grace. This will be a decisive battle for souls.

My Heart bleeds for the souls who will follow the dragon, the beast. Like him, they will be chained in the abyss as the battle ends because in their free will, they decided for darkness and did not choose the Light although the Light chose them. Do not be afraid.

Each soul will have an opportunity to know Me and follow Me even in this time of great persecution because the darkness cannot prevail when a soul seeks True Light. I will provide for My flock. And the fruit of this battle will be a civilization of love. Like the woman who wails in childbirth, the pangs of suffering subside as new life is born. It is the joy of new life that lingers. My sheep who know My Voice are One with My Heart seeing with My Vision. You know that purification is necessary toward the restoration of the world, toward the reconciliation of man with God.

Blessed are you who hear My Voice and follow Me. Remain close together, gathered around your Shepherd and I will lead you to green pastures. Springtime will come for all mankind and My House will by Holy! That is all for now, My lamb. I love you. Your Jesus

106. **4-29-97** Feast of St. Catherine of Siena
Reverence Me in the Eucharist!

Upon receiving Holy Communion I prayed, "I love You, Jesus, through the heart of Mary." Then as soon as I returned to the pew, I became distracted with practical duties to be accomplished today. Firmly, Jesus said: ***Soul! Focus on Me! I will teach you.** Here, I was given an image of a typical modern city scene with many people, very busy, going about their business. In the middle of the scene a Host appeared. Jesus was present but He was restricted, if you will, to a small part of the whole scene.

Jesus said: **This is human vision. My Eucharistic Presence and Love is only a small part in the midst of all the busyness of modern life. Many receive Me in the Eucharist and think of Me for one small moment. Then they go about the rest of the day without another thought of Me.**

Then came an image of the Eucharistic Host which entered into me and went to my heart to remain there. Jesus said: **A true disciple will view everything from the heart because I am there. It is from the heart that I give you to see with My Vision, which is supernatural wisdom. My lamb, view everything from My Body, Blood, Soul and Divinity. Then you will have My Mind, My Heart, My Spirit, My Wisdom for yourself. Then will My Eucharistic Love affect everything that you see and do.**

Eat My Body, Blood, Soul and Divinity to become transfigured into Me. Bring Me into the world. See now, beloved of My Heart, what a treasure you have received, what riches you possess in the Holy Eucharist? Reverence Me!

Tell My people, Jesus is the Eucharist. Come to the Banquet of God! How easily you, My people, forget Me. How unimportant I am to you! I knock and knock at the door of your hearts. I await your response. My lambs, grant Me your love in return. I love you tenderly. Your Jesus

107. **4-29-97 (B)**
Wavering Faith

After Holy Hour I received an image of a tug of war between my will and God's; between my spirit and His. Jesus said: **Your faith moves back and forth because of pride and fear. Today this is true for most people. What obstacles: pride and fear! These overwhelm My people today. Even you who have faith are afraid to walk in that faith, to be courageous and confident in Me.**

Many disciples are afraid of appearing foolish, of being led by the Spirit, becoming a little one of Mine. You are too worried about appearances, reputations and the opinions of others. I am truly a sign of contradiction! But blessed are you who follow the sign of contradiction! You also shall become signs of contradiction for the world. Blessed are you, who embrace the mystery of My Love and become a fool for Me, you shall possess true wisdom. In the end, this will be visible for the world to see.

My bride, do not be afraid to be a fool for Me. Do not waiver back and forth. Allow the Holy Spirit to win the tug of war inside of you. I love you. Your Jesus

108. **4-29-97 (C)**
Humble Yourselves Before God

Then Our Lady began: *My child, on this feast of St. Catherine of Siena, I remind you of my Son's word to Catherine. He told her* **"I am He who is and you are she who is not."**

This is why I have visited the world in these decisive times; to remind the world that God exists and He is true God and you are not. In this time man has made himself a god and he serves only himself. What grave error!

Listen, my children. You exist for God. If you deny this Truth, you will deny yourself eternal life with Him. I come as your Mother, dear children, to remind you that you must become humble before God and serve Him by loving Him and loving one another!

Let Catherine be an example for you. Her little soul was trans-figured into another Jesus for the salvation of the world. From the cell of her little soul, she interceded for all souls and gained merit for the Church. You also are called to be transfigured into another Jesus. But too few are accepting the call.

I remind you, dear little children, you must become humble before God. See yourself in the light of Truth. He is God and you are His creatures. You have dignity because He created you in His image and likeness for Love and eternal Life. If you humble your-selves before him and repent, you will have abundant life. If you continue the present course, denying God and serving yourselves, you will perish in your stubbornness, hardheartedness and pride. I pray for you, for your conversion. I bless you. Your Mother

109. **5-5-97**
Bear Witness

After Holy Communion, I received an image of myself as a prisoner with chains around my ankles and the cell door shut. Jesus said: **Like Paul, you are to bear witness to the Gospel of Love even as you are bound by your current situation. At the moment ordained by the Father, you will be set free from the chains that bind you. Fear Not! I am with you.**

110. **5-6-97**
The Glorious Mysteries in the Light of the Cross

As Father led the Rosary at church for the group, my eyes fixed on the beautiful wooden cross above the altar. Jesus began to relate the cross to each of the Glorious Mysteries.

At the decade of the Resurrection, Jesus said: **My beloved, look at the Lord your God fastened to the wood of the cross for love of you and all humanity. My arms are outstretched, embracing the sacrifice of love, open to all, ready to receive each soul. That you may share in My Resurrection, My Glory, you also must be open to embracing the sacrifice that love re-**

quires; to lay down your life, your human way for the sake of charity for souls.

At the Ascension decade, Jesus said: **That I may lift you up with Me, that you also ascend to the Father, bow your head in humble submission of His Divine Plan for you. That you may be glorified with Me, humble yourself before the Father and trust in His Divine Providence for you and for the world. Whatever sacrifice, whatever is required in your mortal life will bring forth eternal life in Me when united to My Death and Resurrection.**

At the decade of the Descent of the Holy Spirit, Jesus drew my attention to His nakedness on the cross and said: **My beloved, My nakedness is a sign of My willingness to become vulnerable for the sake of love. You also must become vulnerable. Then will My Holy Spirit descend upon you. Love will unite Himself to you on the wood of the cross causing you to be with Me, a co-redeemer of souls. Love will transfigure you into My image. And the cross will not be a stumbling block for you but rather, it will become your victory in Me. Be willing to become vulnerable like Me.**

At the decade of the Assumption of Mary, Jesus pointed out His bare feet nailed to the wood. Then He said: **My beloved, observe My bare feet. Let this be a reminder to you and all disciples that you are barefooted little ones, utterly impoverished except in Me. Look to My Mother, who is your mother. She walked in humility, purity, and obedience that she might glorify the Most Holy Trinity as the first disciple of the Gospel of Love. Imitate her and I will lift you up with her.**

At the decade of the Coronation, Jesus points out the crown of thorns on His Head. He said: **My Mother bore the crown of thorns mystically in her heart. Every disciple will wear the crown of thorns along the journey leading to the crown of glory. The royal road of the cross is the only pathway to glory. Imitate Me and I will cause you to glorify the Father by transfiguring you into Myself.**

My beloved creation, I died for you! I rose from the dead for you! Live in Me. Turn from evil and do good. Humble yourselves and come to Me. I will teach you how to love and have

peace and joy. Glorify Me that I may raise you up with Me. I love you. Jesus

111. **5-7-97**
Two Opposing Armies

During Rosary with Father, I saw the entire world surrounded by an ocean of Divine Mercy. After observing the development of the ocean of grace, I marveled at the immensity of His Mercy. Then I saw the development of war ships upon the ocean; two armadas arose and opposed one another, aiming weapons at each other.

Then angels blew trumpets from the four corners of the earth and war broke out. It was a decisive spiritual battle between good and evil over souls. The enemy ships captured many souls and attempted to carry them away. Then Our Lady said: *Jump into the Ocean of Mercy and you will be saved.*

Then she said: *Little children, God's Divine Grace is ever present and sufficient enough to overcome every evil. One of the most serious evils today is the lie that perpetuates good as evil and evil as good. People are becoming fascinated with evil, especially the youth. Be vigilant, my little ones.*

Strategic tactics for the decisive battle are underway now. When the time comes, there will be many casualties due to the spirit of pride, the lack of repentance and denial of truth. In pride, you will attempt to do everything according to your way and this will take you to the enemy ship leading to perdition. The proud will persecute the humble. But the humble have already found refuge in the vessel of my Immaculate Heart and this is the victorious vessel. Persecution will only serve to increase the fruit of the Spirit in the humble ones.

The ocean of God's Mercy surrounds you, but few avail yourselves of the grace that is offered to you. You have only to accept through repentance and reconciliation. Pray to know God and be receptive to His grace. Implore the Holy Spirit to live in you. Cease to sin. Make peace with one another through forgiveness. Pray to overcome your pride. Pray for the Spirit of truth and acknowledge your lowliness. See the fleeting reality of your mortal existence so that you come to understand the eternal reality of Life in God.

The victory is won in Jesus. But the war over the final destination of souls is still being fought on earth until the final moment. The enemy roams the world now, but not for much longer. He will gather to himself an army of prideful souls who chose the darkness to perpetuate evil lies. Do not give in to his deception that divides by judgement and suspicion.

Put on Love! Love is the light revealing the truth and love is above all. If you seek to do what is necessary to please God; act in charity and grant mercy to those who hurt you. Draw grace from the ocean of Divine Mercy. Come to know Jesus. This happens in prayer from the heart. Dialogue with Jesus. Take time to listen to what He has to say to you. Dispose your hearts to listen more. God speaks of His Love for you directly into your heart. If you pray, you will be very enriched and grow in faith, hope, and love. Thank you for allowing me to assist you on your journey. I love you. Your Mother

112. **5-8-97**
Lamentations

Journal: Prayer. "O my God, Father, Son, and Holy Spirit, my entirety is ravished in pain as I perceive only desolation! I am sinking as if in quicksand; swallowed up in grief; plunged into darkness! Eternal Father, has thou forsaken me? Do You hear the anguished silence of my heart? The sword pierces again and it penetrates deeper with each thrust, tearing my heart apart. In the silence of my mind and spirit, I hear the lamentations of Ezekiel, Jeremiah, and Job; the cry of the psalmist! I echo their anguished plea to You, O God. Have mercy upon my soul! Amen and be glorified!"

113. **5-8-97 (B)**
Sacrificial Lamb

Father prayed over me and I received an image of myself as a little lamb lying on a marble altar. The lamb bled profusely and was close to death. Many angelic beings surrounded the lamb and watched closely. The lamb would be taken to the point of almost expiring because this is what charity of souls called for, almost every drop of blood; a life of sacrifice to draw graces upon those in need of Divine Grace. In this state, the lamb is more spiritually potent, becoming a burnt offering that rises in reparation for sin.

114. **5-13-97**
I Am the Resurrection and Life

There is severe pain across my shoulders and down my back in the form of a cross for two days now. The muscles are tense, the skin tender to the touch. This drains me physically and medicines bring no relief. Father prays and states that I am in intercession for a certain soul. To pray, I must lie flat on the ground.

Prior to praying the Rosary, we prayed over one another to bind any evil spirits. Father was experiencing temptations already, and he did not want to be distracted in the Rosary.

As we bound the evil spirits that were attacking him, I received an image of Our Lady coming to him and she brought a vacuum with her. (An allusion to cleaning a house.) She placed it near Father's head because the evil spirits attack in the mind. She got rid of all of them.

During the Glorious Mysteries at the Apostle's Creed prayer, Jesus said: **I will make the apostles of the latter days, fishers of men.** An image of a fishing boat was given.

At the decade of the Resurrection, I was given images of the resurrected Jesus visiting the disciples, His friends and family after Easter, preceding the Ascension. Each visitation was full of joy, wonder, and awe. Jesus radiated indescribable beauty and glory.

Jesus said: **My beloved creation, I come to you and do not hide from you. I am the Risen Lord and Savior of all. I am the Son of the living God and I come again to you that you may see Me and believe. I promise that springtime will arrive on earth. Love will be resurrected.** (I received an image of the earth in springtime, everything brought to new life. Every nation and people was renewed. The Church displayed an abundance of new life and fruit.)

Jesus continued: **You are living the difficult days of winter. Many are perceiving only darkness. There is much suffering in families and nations. My Sacred Heart is pierced again to observe the persecution of believers and the desolation of non-believers. From My pierced Heart flows the blood and the water of Divine Grace which enables you to endure the long winter, your present trials. Persevere in faith. Come to Me as I come to you. I am the Love that you need. My beloved apostles of the latter days, the time of purification will pass, but the fruit of your suffering will linger. I come to you. See Me! I meet you wherever you are. I come because you are the target of My Love.**

At the decade of the Ascension, I received an image of Jesus ascending into heaven but He did not ascend alone. He drew every man up with Him to go to the Father. It is His Heart that carries us up and to the Father. At the right hand of the Father, He intercedes for all of creation.

At the decade of the Descent of the Holy Spirit, I saw tongues of fire above the heads of people all around the globe. Jesus said: **To combat the evil of the present age, the Holy Spirit descends into the pure hearts of men who are open to receive Him. In these days preceding the great feast of Pentecost, let Me find you praying together in the Upper Room of the Immaculate Heart of Mary. Then you will receive the power of the Holy Spirit that enables you to endure persecution, overcome hardship and persevere in the proclaiming the Gospel of Life.**

On the important feast of Pentecost, gather in prayer with My Mother and receive a great outpouring of the Spirit to increase charity in the world. This grace will manifest in more zeal for souls. The militant Church will be strengthened. There will be more generosity toward the salvation of souls. I will raise up more victim lambs; those willing to surrender completely to be used by Me to save more souls. Let the fire of the Holy Spirit descend upon you as on the first Pentecost and you will be renewed in Him! My blessing in the name of the Most Holy Trinity.

At the decade of the Assumption, I went completely out in prayer.

At the decade of the Coronation of Mary, Father prayed that the Fifth Marian Dogma might be proclaimed and draw many promised graces for the Church. I saw immediately a crown appearing on each person. Mary said: *My Coronation is for every person, a sign of man's dignity before God. When my maternal mediation is proclaimed formally by the Church, you will receive graces from the Two United Hearts; graces that will draw you closer to the truth of God's Love for creation. I, the Mother of all people, embrace each person as a child of the Most High. That universal embrace of Love is part of my maternal mediation.*

Dear children, pray unceasingly with me. In these days of difficulty, you will find peace and joy in my heart where I nourish you and bring you closer to God. Pray for the Church and her Vicar. I love you. Your Mother

115. **5-14-97**
A Praise of Glory: Sr. Elizabeth of the Trinity

I was very touched by Sr. Elizabeth of the Trinity's retreat notes on being a "Praise of Glory" to God and want to meditate upon them. (cf. Eph 1:4-6 and 1:11-12)

"1) A Praise of Glory is a soul that lives in God; that loves Him with a pure and disinterested love without seeking itself.

"2) A Praise of Glory is a soul of silence that remains like a lyre under the mysterious touch of the Spirit.

"3) Silence: inner silence that occurs being centered on God even in the midst of the world.

"4) Praise of Glory is a soul that gazes upon God in faith and simplicity. We don't need to see everything clearly now. Trust constantly. We look at ourselves too much. We want to see and understand. We do not have enough trust in Him who enfolds us in His Love. It is simple.

"5) A Praise of Glory is one always giving thanks. Each of her acts, movements, thoughts, etc., at the same time, are rooting her in love like an echo of the Eternal Sanctus; praise person, thanksgiving person, joyful person.

"6) Praising God for what He has done in us! Christian life is not so much about us doing something for God but praising God for what He has done for us. Eucharist: central to our faith: thanksgiving!

"7) Called to be a Praise for Glory: Christo-centric. Perfect praise of glory: conformed to Jesus' Passion and Death. Love suffering because it makes us like our Spouse.

"We must not stand in front of our cross and examine it closely in itself. But withdrawing into the Light of Faith, we must rise above it and consider it is the instrument of Divine Love!

"A Praise of Glory is communal; a Trinitarian vocation. God does not save us in isolation! God doesn't save us in some abstract, private, ahistorical way, but through the Incarnation of Jesus in time, space, and history, and by sending His Spirit into our hearts crying "Abba, Father" and uniting us into a family – the Church! We are saved as members of the Church: Creed: Communion of Saints.

"To be a Praise of Glory and to be perfectly responsive to the Father's Will, we can never be concerned just about our own personal salvation because God is concerned with the salvation of the whole world. We must have less preoccupation with our private spiritual state and more concern for the salvation of all."

End of Sr. Elizabeth of the Trinity's retreat notes on being a Praise of Glory to God!

116. **5-16-97**
The Promise of a New Pentecost

At Holy Communion, I received an image of the magnificent dove of the Holy Spirit, poised before me with an olive branch in His mouth. I looked at Him and was overcome with love for the Spirit. "O Holy Spirit! How much I love you!" He placed the olive branch, a symbol of peace, into my heart and the image ended.

Jesus said: **Beloved *Soul, receive My Peace. My peace I give to you. Please write for Me and My people.**

Beloved creation, I have said, it is better that I go to the Father, then the Holy Spirit will come to you. He will be your

Advocate. He will bear witness to all that I have taught. You have the Holy Spirit now, the Spirit of Truth; but the spirit of the world has pushed Him out of hearts. The heart is where He dwells, but your hearts are opened to the spirit of the world who leads to death. The Father of all lies leads you down the path of falsehood.

You are living the days of Satan's most blatant attack on souls. Already he is leading a great number into satanic worship, especially the young. Already he has worked secretly sowing seeds of division, immorality, confusion, fear, discouragement, leading to apostasy from the Church, the Truth.

Fear not, My creation, and do not doubt! My covenant stands. The victory is yours in Me. As in the first Pentecost, the Spirit of the Living God will descend upon the world to hearts that are pure, hopeful, and waiting prepared to receive Him and His gifts. The Spirit will keep you in the Truth. He will be your advocate leading you through the most confusing of times.

Faith is waning daily. Cry out with Me to the Father that He will send the Spirit again to renew the face of the earth with a New Pentecost, a fresh outpouring of His Love and gifts.

Pray with Mary in the Upper Room of her Immaculate Heart. The Holy Spirit will descend upon you and you will have power and strength in Him to persevere in the faith, to discern and uphold th Truth, and most importantly, you will have Love. You will be My Presence in a world that persecutes My Holy Name and abolishes My Teachings. Love will empower you to see the Light of Truth in the midst of darkness and you will protect the deposit of faith inside My Church.

The Holy Spirit will lead you into reconciliation with the Father and one another. Love will empower you to forgive those who hurt you and enable you to cease judgement against one another; find the good in your brothers and sisters.

The Holy Spirit empowered the 120 disciples of the early Church gathered in the Upper Room. He will descend upon you and you also will be My witnesses to the ends of the earth. You are charged, My People, with proclaiming the Gospel of Life and can have nothing to do with a culture of death. Never doubt that a New Pentecost will renew the earth. I see your hearts so thirsty for Love, longing for peace. I will fulfill your hearts for I am the Lord, your God and I love you. **Your Jesus**

117. **5-18-97** Pentecost! 12-3AM
Prayer in Desolation

Journal Entry: Desolation! The past week, my spiritual life has been nothing but desolation and severe, oppressive attacks from the devil. I am tormented at night with various temptations against faith and hope. During the day, I battle temptations to futility, aversion to the spiritual life, doubt, confusion, chaos, anger, self-degradation, loneliness, and isolation. These are from the evil one. But God's own Hand tries my soul as I experience His absence and am left in utter desolation in prayer.

Prayer in Desolation:

"O My God, Holy Trinity, You have placed me in the desert and everything in my daily existence serves to plunge me deeper into desolation. I cannot be consoled. Everything hurts! Your absence is like a knife that lacerates my heart. You have placed me in isolation, set me apart in the desert and detached me from everyone.

"O how I thirst for Love! Love so hidden inside me, I cannot perceive You at all! The Spirit of Truth bears witness, You are in me but the spirit of lies assails my mind with thoughts that you have abandoned me. The spirit of Truth whispers to me, 'God will defend you, He will fight for you.' But the spirit of lies yells in my mind, 'Defend yourself, fight for yourself!'

"There is a battle for my soul and I am weary from the battle inside of me. O that I was utterly surrendered! O that I were a child in Your Almighty Hand, resting in Your peace, secure in Your Love. But no, the spirit of the world still influences my reasoning, my actions. I am not yet a little child who trusts. Just when I think I have been crucified and died, this self of mine rises up and seeks to live again.

"Dear God, will this self of mine ever succumb to death while I walk this earth? Grant me this grace, I beg of You! Must I bear this battle inside of me all the days of my life? O how the words of St. Paul echo in my entirety: 'All that I will to do, I cannot do!'"

118. **5-18-97 (B)**
The Spirit of Truth vs. the Spirit of Lies

The Holy Spirit of Truth whispers to me: **Love and forgive your persecutor. Suffer in silence. Do not defend yourself. Let go. Give up control. Seek to be hidden and forgotten. Carry your cross with the courage of a soldier of the King. Walk in the dignity, femininity, purity, and docility of your Mother Mary Most Holy. In the midst of carrying your heavy crosses, do not close in upon yourself, but reach out in charity to every soul. Though your family is in turmoil, look beyond your family and be concerned with the family of God, all mankind. Lay down your life for others. Do not protect yourself, but become vulnerable for the sake of love. When you are hurt, offer up the injustice in silence. Be forgetful of yourself, but do not put yourself down because you are a temple of the Holy Spirit, a house of God.**

Wait upon the Lord. Patience! Overcome your temper with gentleness and kindness. In your suffering, do not compensate or distract yourself. Acknowledge your utter dependence upon God and walk in peace of soul. Be joyful in all your trials and tribulations, because God is the reason for your joy and God never leaves you.

Have hope in the midst of seemingly hopeless situations because God is over the entire world and with Him all things are possible. Never cease praying or you will be disconnected from your lifeline. Battle the devil and his evil temptations. Do not judge. Live in the Truth. Know you are loved. Love is with you, living and creating His beauty in your soul. Light illumines your path. The more difficult the path, the greater the illumination. Do not reason or seek to understand lofty things, but be content to live and love as a child that trusts in His Father.

The spirit of lies (the devil) bombards my mind with these thoughts:

"Correct your persecutor. Retaliate against the one who hurts you. Do not be silent, defend yourself and your family. Take control. Get rid of your cross. Be discouraged. Forget Mary. Take care of yourself. Live and let live. Love hurts. Better to retreat into your-self where it is safe. God does not defend you or your family. Look at the turmoil that He allows to touch you. Do not sacrifice your-self! Enjoy this life and all the world has to offer. Be free from the spiritual life. Carrying the cross is a useless burden. Prayer is a waste of precious time.

"Hurry and enjoy life. You are a fool, incapable of good. Give in to your passions. Feed your ego. Depend upon no one except yourself. Be independent. Evil does not exist. Whatever darkness is in you comes from your past pain and psychological problems. God does not live in you nor will He fight for you. He is far from His people. God's ways are absurd and oppressive. The spiritual life is for priests and nuns. Every one thinks you are a fool to suffer in silence. Suffering is useless. Be angry. You have a right to be. What are you hoping for? Take charge of your life before it's too late."

119. **5-18-97 (C)**
An Attack to Divide

The spirit of division began to plant seeds of doubt about Father's judgement. The enemy began to exaggerate my vulner-ability and perpetuated the lie that it would be best to move away from his direction and go on my own. The more I entertained these temptations, the greater the turmoil inside of me. I became almost paralyzed in the spiritual life.

I distracted myself with shopping and tried to ignore these temp-tations. But I knew something was wrong inside of me. I put it off and avoided looking at this turmoil inside of me. I tried spiritual reading. The enemy did not relent. I began to entertain ways of pulling away from spiritual direction. This was like an agony in-side of me. There was no peace because this was not the Truth but a lie. It wasn't until it was time to pray with Father for a certain soul, that I spoke to him about the temptations.

Over the phone, he prayed for me and bound the evil spirits attacking my soul. When he finished the prayer, immediately I noticed a tremendous difference inside of me. I was "myself" again.

The lie was gone and the Truth reigned. I had peace and joy. The devil attacks the relationship between a soul and its director because he knows that under good spiritual direction, a soul will bear much fruit for the kingdom of God.

120. **5-18-97 (D)**
The Sufferings of an Intercessor and a Special Grace for Pentecost

While reading a spiritual book on Mary, Jesus began to say these words.

My bride, you suffer for the very ones that you love (my family). **More than this, you suffer for the ones that I love** (the family of man). **You suffer for the ones who do not know love and are dying from lack of love.**

Your suffering has meaning that is far reaching because you suffer as My Bride, wedded to the Groom of all souls. We form a covenant of Love for the sake of the salvation of souls. Your burden is not only from the one who betrays and rejects. You suffer another burden that is deeply spiritual and it comes from the Spirit Himself. You are given knowledge, vision to see, to bear the burden of the desolation that exists inside the hearts of men. You share My burden because we are in a union of Love that shares all. So, I give you to see the darkness and it becomes your cross, your burden. You are taking on the desolation of many souls. You weep not for yourself but for everyone and for Me because you love Me and you know that I am Love longing to lavish Myself upon every soul. But you see that few grant Me entrance into their heart. You see the stony hearts of this generation and you bear the frustration of My Own Heart that cannot force itself upon any one, but waits to be invited.

You know the remedy for the desolation of the world, for the spiritual poverty that exists, but you are given to know that man refuses to acknowledge his sickness and sees no need of the medicine that saves. I have allowed you to taste of betrayal, rejection, persecution, discouragement, doubt, fear, futility,

anger, hostility; that you may know your own spiritual poverty and identify with the sufferings of your Groom and those of every victim lamb.

My Bride, when I hide Myself, it is only because I have gone deeper into your soul to draw you deeper into Myself. The deeper I go, the deeper you go and the more sacred a place we enter. It is silent and dark there. But the silence resounds of Love and the darkness is full of Light. I am leading you into deeper holiness – into the realm of the Spirit who is Holy. It is in the realm of the Spirit that union takes place.

You are wearied and bloodied, but your suffering is propelling you into the deeper recesses of My Heart, into the realm of the Spirit, into the Kingdom of the Father. You are sowing in tears, but you will reap in joy. Your spiritual life is full of beauty and goodness and it is a great gift. Your tears of sorrow, your agony of the spirit, will turn into tears of joy and peace. Remain in Me. I, your Lord and Savior, bless you in the name of the Most Holy Trinity and seal you with My Holy Spirit to be Mine as bride and victim forever.

Receive My peace. Allow Me to hold you and cease to resist. I am worthy of your trust. *Soul of My Cross, you would have perished under the weight of this cross if not for My Infinite Mercy. I have rescued you and shall rescue every soul that seeks to be rescued. Your suffering enters into the on going redemption of the world, becoming one with My salvific Passion, Death, and Resurrection.

On this great feast of Pentecost, I confer a special grace upon your soul. You will be My altar. I will set you in the heart of My Church to embellish her with True Love. I grant you the spirit of Mary Magdalene whose love covered a multitude of sin; the spirit of Catherine of Siena whose gifts influenced the Church; the spirit of Teresa (of Avila) whose prayer life caused her to become a spiritual mother to many; and the spirit of Francis (of Assisi) whose purity of heart, zeal for souls, obedience to the Church, and single heartedness won for him a share in My sufferings at Calvary. I have stamped your soul with these spirits that day by day you will grow in the virtues that they lived on their earthly pilgrimage.

Be patient, My bride. The glory of the Father is incomprehensible. To enter into it requires that you die to all that is not holy and rise to all that is holy. You can do nothing except that you must surrender in trust. In docility, you will be led by the Spirit and accompanied by the saints into the very glory of the Father, Son, and Holy Spirit. Blessed are you who wait upon the Lord. *Soul of My cross, grant me your fiat. Bless Me with your little heart and imperfect love. That is all I ask of you. I will do the rest. I love you. Your Jesus

121. **5-18-97 (E)**
Evil Spirits Attack Father

I called Father to thank him for the prayer and tell him of the difference that resulted. He asked for prayer for himself. As he was binding the evil spirits that were attacking his soul, I saw him dressed in warrior's armor. He appeared to be a giant in full armor. Each spirit that was named by him became somehow visible to me, and I observed the dark spirits take a hammer to Father. One by one, the evil spirits began to strike him dealing repeated blows to him. Even though he was a giant, they eventually pounded him into the ground, a little at a time. Their intent was to hammer him all the way into the ground, to get rid of him completely. By the time Father finished binding the spirits, the scene changed.

I saw a crown of thorns radiating with light. Because God had fashioned it, it was a gift of union. I observed Jesus place it upon Father's head and he bled. Then I saw myself standing next to Father, and Jesus placed a similar crown of thorns upon me. Then He placed a ring on our fingers; a sign that we belonged to the family of the Father.

I saw that Jesus had placed a type of chain around us, binding us to Himself so that no enemy could steal us away. The chain was Divine Love, and it cannot be broken except by our own free will, which could refuse it. This chain of love bound us to our Savior and we were secure in it. Jesus led the way and we followed behind him, side by side, two by two.

Suddenly, the heavy cross of man's sins appeared and rested upon the shoulders of Jesus. We helped to carry it as we walked behind Him along an uphill path. The dove of the Holy Spirit descended upon all three of us. We walked, slowly but surely, with Jesus, carrying the cross along a difficult path, but empowered by the grace and light of the Holy Spirit.

122. **5-18-97 (F)** Pentecost Sunday
The Triumph of the Two Hearts

During the Rosary with Father, I went into a prayer state in which I heard or saw nothing until the fifth decade. Then I saw the image of Our Lady of Lourdes with emphasis on her hands folded together in prayer, a gesture imploring more prayer. Then the image included the grotto of Lourdes. As she stood in the grotto she said: *I appeared at Lourdes to ratify the Church's proclamation of the dogma of the "Immaculate Conception", bringing forth a spring of living water to heal the people of God. This was a gift from God bestowed upon the world as the Church had defined the truth about my Immaculate Conception. The Spirit leads the Church to proclaim and define Truths to bring blessings upon the entire Mystical Body of Christ.*

When the Church gives a dogmatic definition of my maternal roles of Co-Redemptrix, Mediatrix, and Advocate for the people, the Father will ratify the Church's teaching and the floodgates of grace will flow through my Immaculate Heart into the hearts of people. There will issue forth a new wellspring of living water to heal the nations. Pray for this intention which will facilitate the Triumph of the United Sacred and Immaculate Hearts.

Here I asked Our Lady, "My Mother, what is meant by the Triumph of Your Two Hearts?

Daughter, the triumph of the Immaculate Heart will be when the serpent's head is crushed by my heel. When the menace of evil is banished from the earth, the Two Hearts will reign because man's heart will see the Truth, have the Spirit of Love, and knowledge of the Father. God's creation will truly be "Children of the Most High." Offer prayer and sacrifice for this intention. I love you. Your Mother

123. **5-19-97**
Support John Paul II

During the Rosary with Father, I went out in prayer but at the end I received an image of Pope John Paul II walking the Via Dolorosa with a huge cross upon his shoulders. The Church was the cross; the burden he carries, for love of it. Suddenly, people came forward to assist him to carry the cross.

Our Lady said: *Your prayers, sacrifices, and sufferings, serve to assist my beloved son, the Vicar of Christ, in carrying the weight of the cross. The Church is being attacked from within and without. The spiritual darkness of this age is a burden upon him. He is one with my sorrowful heart, keenly aware of the sufferings of man and willing to bear the burden for many. Pray for him. I implore you little children, pray for him. He is bringing blessings upon the world through his sacrifice. Support him! I love you. Your Mother*

When Father prayed for the proclamation of the dogma of Mary, Co-Redemptrix, Mediatrix, and Advocate, I saw the globe of the earth. Suddenly the Crown of Jesus, the King, and Mary, the Queen, intertwined together and seven crowns appeared over seven continents. Brilliant rays of divine grace poured down from the crowns to the continents.

124. **5-26-97**
To Serve Him

On the plane to Europe for a conference in Rome, Jesus said to me: *Soul of My Cross, thank you for your sacrifice. I am pleased that you are willing to forfeit your will for Mine. This draws inestimable graces upon your soul. You serve Me, not as a slave, but as one who loves Love. You are leaning on Me. Continue! I am with you and you are in Me. My Peace. I love you. Jesus*

125. **5-28-97** Rome
Place All of Your Confidence in Me!

Father and I went to the Church of the Holy Spirit near St. Peter's Square in Rome. It is here that Pope John Paul II, on April 25, 1995, venerated and enthroned the Image of Jesus of Divine Mercy, which now occupies a side altar. There is also a large painting of Blessed Faustina and the Sisters from her Order are the caretakers of this Church. We attended Holy Mass and remained to pray the Rosary together with devotions to Our Lady of Fatima. The priests venerated a large statue of Our Lady of Fatima and processed around the church while the congregation sang Marian Songs. Most beautiful!

Following the services, we knelt in prayer at the side altar of Divine Mercy. I said to Jesus, "My Lord and Savior, have mercy on me, a sinner. I kneel before You to thank You for bringing me here to this holy ground. Thank You for leading us to this Church of the Holy Spirit where the Holy Father has enthroned You as Jesus of Divine Mercy. I bring before You, my husband and children." Immediately Jesus said: **Would you bring to Me only your husband and children? Rather, bring to Me all husbands and wives, and all children, all mothers and fathers, and brothers and sisters. Bring them all to Me. Implore My Mercy for all of them. Do this for Me, *Soul, My bride and victim lamb.**

Now, look at the words below My Image of Divine Mercy. What do they say, *Soul?

They say, "GESU CONFIDO IN TE"; Confidence, Jesus, trust in You.

Yes, soul. Place all of your confidence in Me. Pray for every family. All are in need of My Mercy. Families are especially targeted by Satan. It is My Spirit that binds the family together. But many families do not know or welcome the Spirit. You are drawing Divine Grace upon all families. Place all of your confidence in Me. I will never forsake families!

I can unite what is divided. My Spirit will come to the aid of families that welcomes Me. Pray that families are willing to receive My Spirit of Love that unifies. Families are breaking

apart because of selfishness. A whole generation had been raised to be self-centered and self-indulgent. Now families are suffering the effects of the absence of sacrificial love. I have chosen many victim souls to facilitate the healing of families.

Place all of your confidence in My merciful Heart. Offer to Me your own rejection, betrayal and humiliation and I will bring forth new life for families. Thank you, My bride and victim, for your love. Peace. I am with you. Your Jesus

126. **5-29-97** Rome, Hotel Columbus, My room 5:30AM.
Defend the Cross and the Eucharist

At 5AM I heard: "Please write." I resisted. Again I heard: "Please write." I knew this was not Our Lord or Our Lady. I asked: "Who is speaking to me?" I heard interiorly, "Enduring Love." The special angel whom the Father gave to me was beckoning me.

I began to see the following image, vividly. I saw the globe of the earth suspended in space. Then I saw the heavens above full of light. The cross of Jesus appeared atop the globe of the earth and it spanned between earth and heaven. Jesus was on the cross. Then I was given to see into the bowels of the earth. There was a force there that seemingly pulled down the cross with great rapidity. It was as if the earth swallowed up the crucifix. The cross of salvation could no longer be seen having seemingly disappeared.

Suddenly I saw myself, Father, and many other Christians descend to the bowels of the earth. We grasped the crucifix and altogether pushed it up and out of the earth so that it appeared again on earth and spanned to the heavens. It was a small but mighty army that accomplished this.

Our Lady said: *My children, the theologians*, intellectuals*, and men of the world of great power will not do this.* (Allusion to the image of putting the cross back into place.) *The little ones will do it. The little ones will do it!* (She repeated). *Pause.*
(*Those theologians/intellectuals who have no Love.)

There is an unbloody war, more dangerous than a bloody war. (Allusion to Hitler, World War II, - the history I was reading at 3AM.)

My children, your eyes cannot behold this unbloody war. It is spiritual. It is for souls. It is far more dangerous because it is hidden from your eyes and you need the vision of the Holy Spirit to "see" it, to "know" it.

This unbloody war has already claimed many souls. The evil spirit has a foothold in the Mystical Body of Christ. Satan seeks to undermine the faith of the Roman Catholic people. This is a sword piercing my maternal Heart now.

The hour is very late, my children. Many have already lost their faith in Jesus. Many have abandoned the Church, her precepts, and her sacraments. Many refuse my maternal grace; grace that comes from the Holy Spirit. The Great Apostasy is well underway. Without the grace that comes through the Church, through the sacraments and prayer, more souls are very vulnerable to the deception of the enemy. O how he targets the Roman Catholic Church!

Jesus is the head. Satan seeks to seduce the body away from the head. The army of Satan seeks to subvert my Son, Jesus, the cross of salvation, and the Eucharist! Satan seeks to cause doubt, disbelief in the cross of salvation and in the Bread of Life (Eucharist). He has his own army that has worked secretly toward this.

There is an army of souls gathered in my Immaculate Heart prepared to defend the cross of salvation; prepared to protect the Eucharist. These souls are the apostles of the latter days leading to a new era, a civilization of love. These apostles will pray and fast and sacrifice, lay down their lives for souls and call down a New Pentecost through the Church and for the world. The Holy Spirit of God leads these souls. His love burns in their hearts. His Light illumines their path and in their nothingness, these servants of God, children of my Immaculate Heart, will be raised up. And as they are raised up, they will hold the cross of salvation up high. It will span from the earth to the heavens.

Again, by means of the cross, many will be saved from the lies and seduction of the enemy. Know, my dear children, he wants no soul for himself. He hates every soul. He wants souls because they belong to Jesus. He seeks to take them from Our Savior. That is his only goal. Therefore, be vigilant and pray as much as possible. And it is possible to pray always. Peace. I love you. Your Mother

127. **5-31-97** Domus Mariae, Rome conference, Latin Mass with Fifty Bishops
The Visitation: Support for the Holy Father

At Holy Communion Our Lady said: *Blessed are you, my beloved children, gathered together at the Eucharistic table, offering the Perfect Sacrifice of Our Jesus to the Heavenly Father in the Holy Spirit and through my maternal Immaculate Heart. O how I love you, my little children!*

What incomprehensible graces are yours today as you intercede for Christ's Vicar and the Mystical Body! It is my joy to be in your midst. It is my joy to run with haste to each of you, to carry Jesus to you, to bless you by the power of the Holy Spirit, to rejoice with you! Pray with me these words, "He who is Mighty has done great things for me. Holy is His Name!"

The family of this movement has become a support, a blessing for His Holiness, John Paul, the Peter of this present age. While the spirit of the world hurls darts at him, while those in his own household await his demise, you form a spiritual shield for him. Your prayers and sacrifices serve to inflame his heart with love and fortify his spirit with graces of perseverance and courage. You are his hope for this Church! This is possible because you exist in my Immaculate Heart by means of your consecration. And my Immaculate Heart envelops him.

Little ones, you cannot comprehend the scope of your mission, the fruit of which will remain long after your days on earth are passed. Unite in my heart. Prostrate in prayer. Love and support one another. I love you. Your Mother

128. **6-1-97** Feast of Corpus Christi, Rome Conference, My room.
Corpus Christi, the Eucharist and Mary

My beloved children,
Feast on My Body and Blood! It is Life for your soul! Partake of Me! Come! Be one with Me! I remain with you in this humble Sacrament of Love. Take and eat My Body, Blood, Soul and Divinity! I am for you! Be for Me! Love longs to love you. Why do you hesitate to love Me? Are you afraid of Love Him-

self? Perhaps what Love will require? Truly I say to you, beloved ones, do not hesitate. Run to Me! Come empty! I will fill you and teach you to love correctly.

What do I require? A sacrifice indeed! The sacrifice consists of an exchange. My Perfection for your imperfection; My Life for your death; My Divinity for your humanity; My Truth for your falsehood; My Peace for your confusion; My Infinite Love for your emptiness; My Humility for your pride; My Joy for your sadness; My Friendship for your loneliness; My Courage for your fear; My Strength for your weakness; My Wisdom for your reasoning; My Fullness for your desolation!

Great is My offer. Yet more people refuse it. I am a patient and persistent lover of souls. I will never cease to invite you, to beckon you unto Myself that we may exist in a relationship of love, eternally.

Be forewarned. The longer you delay the greater your desolation. All men seek love, peace, and joy. I alone provide it. I am Love, peace, joy, Life! Your delay wounds My tender Heart because it hurts you. Without Me, you are terribly wounded. You are vulnerable to every kind of sin. Sin wounds you mortally, extracting True Life from your soul. Cease to sin and do not resist Me! Do not delay! Come. Eat and drink of your Lord and Savior! The Bread I give to you is Life for the world. (Jn)

Bring Life into the world. Allow My Body, Blood, Soul and Divinity to transfigure you into another sacrament of love; another sacrifice for the world. Come. Receive the first share of your inheritance. Life! Union! Approach My Eucharistic Altar daily. As you ingest daily bread for your body, ingest daily Bread for your soul. Love awaits you at the Altar of Sacrifice.

Blessed are you gathered together in intercession for the papal definition of the whole truth about Our Mother's maternal mediation. I am with you interceding to the Father for such a grace to come upon the world, for all people, through My Mystical Body by the hand of My Vicar. The Immaculate Heart surrounds you. You are bathed in grace today. You are calling down grace for My Vicar and My Mystical Body. I bless you in incomprehensible ways. You are forming a family, uniting My Mother's remnant army. My peace I give to you.

Be prepared to battle the opposition; to be persecuted, ridiculed, rejected by many in the world. Respond in humility, peace, and love. Serve My Church in her hour of greatest need. Remain in the truth of your nothingness. Then can My Holy Spirit fill you with His Power. True Wisdom from the Spirit comes to a humble, detached heart. Seek Wisdom's vision through the Eucharist, constant prayer, fasting, and reparation. Together, My Holy Spirit and My Mother, will teach you to work, to prepare the way for the Triumph of the Immaculate Heart leading to the reign of My Eucharistic Heart in a civilization of love.

The Father is pleased with your offering; these days of prayer and teaching. You have honored Me by honoring the Immaculate Heart of Mary. She is My gift to you, the masterpiece of the Most Holy Trinity, full of grace for you. Mother of the Eucharist embraces you in her maternal love. She suffers, nourishes, and pleads for you.

Pray very much for your brothers and sisters who do not welcome her maternal mediation. The enemy has a hold of many in the Church who oppose all that you work toward. Persevere. You, the few, will claim victory. Many victim souls are needed!

Are you willing to drink of the chalice of suffering? Remember, Calvary procured the victory of Resurrection. The Eucharist will fortify you. Be vigilant. Satan will target all those called to uphold Mother Mary and the Holy Sacrifice of the Mass, the Eucharist. This is My Covenant. By these two (Mary and the Eucharist), you will be restored in faith, hope, and love. Fear not! I am with you. My Peace I give to you. Please continue to dedicate prayers for My Vicar. Your Jesus

129. **6-2-97** On Airplane home from Rome Conference
Convert Again and Wait on the Lord!

I was trying to sleep when Our Lady said: *Child, please write for the Prayer Group.*

My beloved children,

I bless you in the name of the Most Holy Trinity. Thank you for allowing me to teach you. Always together, the Holy Spirit and I have knocked on the door of your hearts continuously over the years.

The Father Almighty sent me to the world to implore His people to convert, to pray. Many heeded my messages. Prayer cenacles formed throughout the world. Whenever you gather to pray the Rosary, I am there to pray with you. I see that the fervor of the early years of conversion has waned for some. This is true for some of the family I have gathered in my Immaculate Heart. (I believe Our Lady refers to the Marian Movement.)

I see your weariness. You persevere, thanks be to God. But you are questioning your call; dissecting the graces and growing impatient and doubtful of the prophecies that you have heard from different prophets about the future of the world. Humanly, you thought some of these prophecies would come to pass by now. I remind you, beloved children, your timing is not God's timing. His is Perfect!

Little ones, do not give into human reasoning above faith in God. Please do not break faith. So much is happening that you cannot see. Now is not the time to grow weak in faith, hope, and love. Now is the time to pray more than ever, to persevere toward Union with God, to fortify your soul with the Body and Blood of my Son, to increase in zeal for souls, to battle courageously against the enemy, the spirit of the world.

Blessed are you who believe! Recall your enthusiasm to be a soldier for Jesus? I was sent to you, to the world, by the Father and the Son. In the power of the Holy Spirit, I came to knock on the door of your heart. And you responded! Joyfully! You heeded my messages. You toiled without considering the cost.

You believed in the spirit of prophecy. The spirit of prophecy forewarned you of these days of trial, persecution, dryness, these days of walking the Via Dolorosa. The spirit of prophecy said, "You will endure all that Jesus endured." Gather inside my Immaculate Heart to pray, offer reparation for the sins of the world, and together you will battle and be victorious. All soldiers grow weary. You must be fortified continuously because the battle is constant.

Prayer fortifies; the Sacraments replenish. But many are expending energy in worry, doubt, reasoning (wanting to know and understand), *fear, confusion. If you take your eyes off Jesus, this will happen to you.*

Inside my Immaculate Heart, too many are looking at themselves or to others. My Immaculate Heart if full of the Holy Spirit. You have only to rest there, breathe the Spirit of the Living God there. Allow the Holy Spirit to permeate your entirety. The Holy Spirit is always creating. Love is creative. The Holy Spirit works in your soul to create Beauty; to make you beautiful like Him. God is always with you. When you take the time to be with Him, you cooperate with His Grace and Presence. You are blessed most whenever you give God "freedom" in you. He will fortify you with His own strength. He will grant you His Peace and increase your faith.

Now is the time for you to be built up in love. Build one another up. The days to come will bring many trials for mankind. Purification of the world is part of the Triumph of my Immaculate Heart. Purification serves to sanctify. You are being transfigured into my Son to be His Presence in the world. Thank you for surrendering. I take all your intentions, burdens, prayers, sacrifice, to the throne of Our Triune God. He receives them and grants everything in accordance with His Perfect Divine Will, in His perfect time. I implore you gathered in my Immaculate Heart, convert again!! I love you. Your Mother

130. **6-2-97(B)**
Hold Onto Me!

On the airplane from Rome to USA, I began to have what I will call a spiritual panic attack about coming home to a difficult situation. I became preoccupied with escaping from pain, rejecting any more suffering. The revulsion for suffering increased and even seemingly caused me to have physical manifestations such as tightness of breathing, constriction of muscles etc. It was intense and I began to experience claustrophobia for the first time on an airplane. Tears spontaneously began and it took all of my effort to keep my composure. Just when I was going to ask Father for prayer,

Jesus said in a very firm tone: **Hold onto Me!** These words came so powerfully that they resounded throughout my being and the tears ceased, the muscles relaxed and I was still, instantly!

Jesus continued: **Hold onto Me!** This time His words were accompanied with a vivid vision. I saw Jesus, very bloodied, very beaten, exhausted, walking and carrying a very huge wooden cross on one shoulder. The weight of the cross caused Him to be stooped down, almost falling onto the ground. I could see vividly, His sweat, the bloodied wounds, and the heavy cross digging into His back and shoulders.

Then I saw that the vertical cross beam had the name of my husband carved on it and the horizontal cross beam had the names of our children carved on the left and right side. I saw myself in the scene, very bloody and beaten down. I wore a crown of thorns that bled profusely and was barely able to walk anymore, still trying to carry the cross with Jesus, however. But in my weakness, Jesus had to hold me up with His right arm while carrying the cross of the family with His left arm.

Immediately I said, "Jesus! It seemed to me that I was carrying the cross by myself. I did not perceive that you were carrying it along with carrying me! When I observe your own tears in sympathy with mine, I am surprised! But why should I be? Did I not realize the depth of Your compassion for me and my family?

"O my God! How unreal this seems and yet how vivid it is. Perhaps I am taking a flight from reality to ease my pain. Jesus, how do I know that the spiritual life inside of me is real?"

*Soul of My cross, the Holy Spirit of Truth bears witness in your soul to the reality of Divine Grace in you. Are you not at peace now? How is it that you are steady now? It is I who have rescued you!

The supplications of your heart are known to Me! I am with you always; not sometimes, not only when you are in need of Me or call on Me, but always, everywhere! Have I not said, "We are one heart?" When you bleed, I bleed. When you weep, I weep. Whatever is done unto you is done unto Me. You are never alone! There are times such as now that I break through the silence of our union to reassure you that I am with You! I am fighting for you, defending you. My Word is true! My Cov-

enant everlasting! What I provide for you no human being can provide for you. Again, I have rescued your tormented mind, your broken heart and healed you. Be healed, My beloved one! In Me you are made well and whole. Whatever the world takes from you, I will replace with something far more excellent! Again, I say to you, hold onto Me! I will carry you and your family home. Trust Me. I love you. Jesus

131. 6-3-97
More Temptations

It is as if the evil spirits repeatedly play a tape in my mind that says, "Take control of your life. You know that you want your old life back." This never ceased all day long until Father prayed over the phone and bound and cast out the evil spirits. Then the temptations ended.

132. 6-4-97
The Healing Power of the Word of God!

When I arrived for morning Mass, I was filled with grief for our family. The reading at Mass from *Tobit* really touched and healed me. The readings spoke of how Tobit was despairing because of health problems. He prayed that God would take his breath away, that he would die. Then they spoke of Sarah who was despairing because of false accusations against her. She intends to hang herself in her room but at the last moment decides against this so as not to disgrace her father.

Both of these poor souls turn to God in prayer. And the Scripture tells us that their prayers were heard as they entered the heavens, entered God's Glory. And God answered them. He sent the Archangel Raphael, which literally means, "God heals." Rafael goes to Tobit, to Sarah, to heal them and their despair is gone.

I also received a healing through these readings. God's grace overcame me and all the grief and discouragement lifted. What power in the Word of God!

133. **6-5-97**
On Marriage and Family

After Mass and Holy Hour, Our Lady spoke regarding the first reading about Tobiah taking Sarah as his wife.

Daughter, Tobiah takes Sarah as his wife and immediately turns to God with supplications that He (God) be the center of their marriage. Marriage is a sacrament that is a covenant between three persons, God, husband and wife.

Unless God is included in the sacramental relationship, the spirit of the world will seduce husband away from wife or wife away from husband. The Sacrament of Marriage is a holy covenant, a reflection of God's love for creation. It is a covenant that yields the fruit of love, children. It requires sacrificial love, an act of total self-donation, a dedication of oneself to the welfare of the family. The family is a God-given, God-chosen, gift of Love. It is within the family that Love is learned and exchanged. This is life. God must be the center of it because only the family of Father, Son, and Holy Spirit can unite families in their perfect love.

The breakdown of families is precisely because God has been removed from the center of life. In His place, men, women, and children have erected a temple to themselves. Wherever self-idolatry exists, there is self-indulgence and a turning away from self-sacrifice. A family does not exist where people live in a house but dedicate themselves to their own respective welfare, forgetful of one another, negligent of relationship with one another.

The union of man and woman in the Sacrament of Matrimony is truly beautiful. This is God's design, reflecting His Own Divine Love and Beauty. Today, however, men and women are making a mockery of the Sacrament of Marriage. The fidelity required in this sacrament can only be fulfilled through fidelity to God and His precepts. Grace is needed for faithfulness, but sin is a barrier to grace. Therefore, avoid sin and sinful situations. Avail yourselves of the sacraments and pray for your marriage, your partner and the family. Bring God into everything.

Today, the spirit of the world targets marriages to cause the breakdown of families. Why? Because with the breakdown of families comes the breakdown of love. And with the breakdown of love comes every kind of evil and the breakdown of nations and churches. Evil erects itself as the god of the world.

Whenever the Father, Son, and Holy Spirit are banished from a soul, a family, or a nation, Satan erects an altar to the self. Satan knows that human pride desires this. And often this is done under the guise of a good. Pride is unable to detect itself! This is why so many marriages and families are falling apart.

Like Tobiah and Sarah, men and women must humble themselves before God and pray. With supplications from the heart, they must declare their mutual dependency upon the Triune God and seek every Divine Grace available to remain faithful – to God, to themselves and their covenant meant to be holy! The union of man and woman is made in heaven! It must be sustained by all that is heavenly and holy!

Implore the Holy Spirit of Truth to guide your soul, your marriage, and your families. He gives the Light to detect sin and selfishness, which leads to infidelity. Resist the demon of self-idolatry.

When you defend your family and remain faithful to your marriage covenant, you are in fact upholding God's Love and the world is blessed. Whenever the devil tempts you away from your families, your spouse, he is seducing you away from the Truth, playing on your emotions.

Love is an act of the will, a decision, not a feeling. Where there is love, there is a sacrifice of self for the sake of another. This sacrifice is precisely what brings true joy in loving, it is the giving, the gift of self.

Whatever you deny yourself in this life, so fleeting, whatever sacrifice is required to remain faithful to your marriage and family, will bear fruit that endures forever and amass a treasure for you in the next life. Only in the next life will your joy be complete.

It is a serious offense against God and the family of man to break your marriage covenant and break up a family. If you could see all the hearts torn asunder because of selfish acts of infidelity, you would weep with me! My maternal heart bleeds profusely as this sword pierces me continuously.

Turn to Me, all of you who suffer the breakdown of the family. I suffer with you. Allow Me to be your consolation. Turn to the Father, Son, and Holy Spirit who are full of compassion for you.

Enter into the family of the Holy Trinity through my heart and you will never be forsaken.

I implore you, dear children, to pray very much for marriages and families because Satan's arrows are aimed at them. I love you. Your Mother

134. **6-5-97(B)**
On the Greatest Commandment

Beloved people,

It is written, the most important commandment consists of loving Me with all of your heart, soul, mind, and strength. Secondly, love one another! How many are truly keeping this commandment? I say to you, only a remnant! My foremost commandment is for your good. If you live it, it will make you free to soar to the heights of love. If you do not live it, you will suffer under the oppressive chains of the spirit of the world. You will suffer the absence of love.

Know that My commandments are for your good. If you are for Me, you will be free on earth and in heaven. If you are for yourself first, you will not know freedom, but will be a slave to yourself. Love will elude you. Know that My commandments are for your good and keep them for love of Me. I love you. Jesus

135. **6-6-97** Feast of the Sacred Heart of Jesus
Do not Mock My Sacred Heart

At Holy Communion, I saw the Sacred Heart of Jesus in the form of an enormous human heart, all aflame, a roaring fire, radiating heat and light, full of Power and Majesty! O how I desired His Heart to consume me! Then I was given to see a small sphere lodged toward the bottom of this magnificent, living Heart of Love. It was the globe of the earth. I thought, "How small the globe is compared to this Heart of Love."

Jesus said: **Know, child, that My Sacred Heart envelops all of creation. See the proper perspective of Life. See that the Infinite Divine Love of the Holy Trinity is the everlasting reality. My Heart is man's true home. Your life on earth is vital because it is the beginning of your pilgrimage to Me. But it is small compared to the eternal relationship of Love to which you are called and for which you are created.**

Therefore, child of Mine, keep your sufferings in the proper perspective. Do not become overwhelmed by them. They will pass. Everything on earth will pass. Keep focused on the Eternal Three, Father, Son, and Holy Spirit.

On this feast of My Sacred Heart, give thanks to the Father who sent Me, who ordained My human heart. Give thanks to My Mother, whose Immaculate Heart, by the power of the Holy Spirit, formed the Incarnate Word, for you, for all.

My Sacred Heart burns with Love for all creation. Yet it is little loved in return. Satan has caused many to make a mockery of Love. Let this Sacred Heart of Mine enter you to reveal the Truth that Love exists for you!

Your mockery of Me wounds Me because it is a degradation of yourself. Your dignity comes from Me, and the Father, and the Holy Spirit. When you mock He who dignifies you, you degrade yourself. This is precisely what Satan wants you to do. He tears down. I lift up! Love lifts you up unto Himself.

How do you mock Me? When your faith in Me is but a pretense; when you offer lip service once a week; when your hope is in yourself; when you refuse to sacrifice for the sake of true love; when you live independent of Me; ignore My promptings and precepts; exist in indecision, lukewarmness; you mock Me, you deny Me.

Cease to resist. Come unto Me. I will reveal true life and love to you. Take this Heart of Mine and make it your own. That is why My Divinity took on your humanity; to show the Way, the Truth, the Life, to lead you home. Come. Invoke this Heart of Mine and it will be ours. I love you. Your Jesus

136. **6-6-97 (B)** At Prayer Group on the Feast of the Sacred Heart
The Sacred Heart Encourages

My little ones,

It is with great joy that I give to you My Sacred Heart of Love. This is what I do for love of you. You have My Sacred Heart inside of you. Remember always, walk in My Love and Holiness. While I thirst for love still, I am consoled to receive your love as you pray this night. The Most Holy Trinity is with you. Offer gratitude on this special feast of My Sacred Heart to the Eternal Father. He so loved the world, His creation, that He sent His Only Son to live with you, to die for you and to rise again for you. The Father is Love Incomprehensible. To Him be the Glory, Praise and Thanksgiving!

Thank you for inviting the Holy Spirit to descend into your heart to reveal the Truth of My Love that burns for you. My Covenant of Love will uphold you through the most trying of times. Please trust that I will never forsake you. You have glorified My Sacred Heart as you gathered to pray the Rosary in intercession with the Immaculate Heart. You have received many graces from the Heart of Love.

Through the consecrated hands of My priest, through the blessed oil, you have been anointed again to fulfill your ministry of Love, interceding for the salvation of the world. You received images of life and death, of joy and suffering. All these bear the fruit of Love and the grace of conversion. Thank you for offering yourselves to be intercessors for the world. Your prayer is powerful and far-reaching. I bless you from the depths of My Sacred Heart. I love you tenderly, mercifully, and infinitely. Your Jesus

137. **6-7-97** Feast of Immaculate Heart of Mary. My prayer room.
The Secret of Mother Mary's Faith, Hope, Love

Journal entry: I was busy doing domestic chores all day and didn't leave the house until 7:30PM for evening Mass. I was alone all weekend because the rest of the family is out of town. It wounds my heart that my family is so often scattered. As the children get older, it seems we have less time together. The cherished years of their childhood pass so quickly. A mother suffers this.

By Holy Communion time, I had a terrible headache and could barely remain in the Church. This wore me down very quickly. When I received Holy Communion I prayed, first in thanksgiving to Jesus and then to my Mother Mary.

"O Mother Mary, on this feast of your Immaculate Heart, please help your daughter! How I need you to be my mother! Press my sorrowful heart, the heart of a mother, into your Immaculate Heart of pure love and wisdom. Let me rest there. O how I hurt! Through and through I am full of pain. O Mary, hold me close to your heart. Embrace me with your love, I beg you! Teach me, please. How do I love as you do? How can I be a mother like you? A spouse like you? O Mary, my Mother, I want to ponder your ways because from your little Holy Family in Nazareth to the entire family of man, you are MOTHER!

You are reconciler, unifier, healer, servant, humble, joyful, peaceful, loving! Teach me, O Mother of God, Mother of mine, how to imitate you! Mary Most Holy, I need you to help me to keep loving in the face of betrayal, abandonment, rejection, indifference, persecution, even malice aimed at me. O Mary, at the foot of the cross, your hope was greater than the darkness! Hold me please, my Mother, and whisper to me, the way to have hope in the midst of a seemingly hopeless situation that confronts my family. What is the secret Mother Mary to your faith, hope, and love, there at the foot of the cross, when all that you were told seemed to be contradicted? In that chaotic moment of darkness, it would appear that Jesus had been defeated. But you knew that was not the Truth. What is the secret to your wisdom, Mother of mine? And how can it be mine?

I heard: *Grace, grace, grace. I received the grace to consent fully, freely, promptly, continuously to God's Divine Will. That is the secret to inner peace that comes from God. That is the secret to faith in the midst of contradicting situations; to hope in the midst of seemingly hopeless situations; to love in the midst of terrible atrocities against love.*

Daughter, consent fully, freely, promptly, continuously to God's Will. You will know it by the power of the Holy Spirit of Truth in your soul. When your life is reconciled with God, when it is in right order, a Godly order, you have the Spirit of Truth to illumine your mind, heart, and will to walk in the Light of God's Divine Plan for you and Wisdom will not remain apart from you. Wisdom from the Holy Spirit, flowing through my Heart, will guide every decision of your life, if you but consent freely, fully, promptly, continuously to the Divine Will of God.

This is not the antidote to suffering. But it is the secret to endure all suffering, contradictions and defeat, in the light of faith that believes in God; that brings good out of suffering; in the light of hope that pierces the darkness of hopeless situations; and in the light of love that is more powerful than any darkness.

My little child, I have shared my secret with you. Furthermore, often as you come to me, I will assist you to hold onto the secret, embrace it, and live it.

I love being your Mother! Do you love it when your children come to you in distress, in need, so little and poor, and you as mother console, help, and heal them by your love for them? I, too, love being a Mother who consoles, helps, and heals. And the quickest way that I can do this is by taking you to the Heart of Jesus. While I am the vessel of His Grace, not passive, but active, He is the Giver, the Creator of all Divine Grace.

To all God's children I implore you, please allow me to be your Mother. I long to unite you, heal you, console you. Most of all, I want to reconcile you to God. He is your Love, Peace, Joy. He is Life for you. Let us be a true, loving family. I love you. Your Mother

138. **6-11-97**
The Bleeding Heart: Sacrifice of Love

During the Rosary with Father, at the Resurrection decade I received an image of Jesus placing His Hand on my heart and in it was a surgeon's scalpel. He seemingly made an incision with the scalpel and caused my heart to bleed. He said: **Bleed for Me, My lamb. Bleed for Me, My bride. Bleed for Me, My victim. Open up your heart. Do not close it! Do not let it become hard. Do not block out Love. Allow Love to come to you. Open up! Con-**

tinue to love in spite of the malice that comes at you. Never cease to love. I will see to it, Myself, that you remain open to Love. Bleed for Me, little lamb. Bleed for souls, little victim.

Your little heart must not become cold, hard, or fearful, though it is assailed with tortuous blows. I will not allow it! I have given you My Heart. Your heart must never succumb to anything less than Love. And My Love in you is noble and everlasting, for I am Perfect Love. Love has wounded your heart that you will continue to love, especially to love enough to forgive those who have torn you heart apart.

It is I who allow you to endure a type of crucifixion. You must do so with a singular disposition to grow in love! We are one Heart, bleeding together and loving together. You are not alone. I am with you to keep you alive to Love. Be comforted in Me. Bleeding signifies the sacrifice of love. Peace. I love you. Jesus

139. **6-11-97 (B)**
Enemies of the Church

At the end of the Rosary with Father, I saw St. Peter's Basilica in Rome and the entire Vatican City. On Via Conciliazoni, the street leading to the Piazza of St. Peter's, I saw an army marching. The army had red uniforms, marching with great precision, and their faces were determined, strong, and serious. They continued to march all along Via Conciliazoni until they got to the Piazza of St. Peter's where they seemed to disappear altogether from sight. It was as if a secret underground passage led them out of sight, underground of St. Peter's Basilica. It was underground that they worked. In secret, they plotted out a strategy of some kind.

Our Lady began: *The red army signifies high level Freemasonry working to undermine the authority of the Holy Father, the authority of the Roman Catholic Church. They plot to undermine the three-year plan set forth by the Pope for the Church, the preparations leading to the Jubilee Year (2000). My beloved son, John Paul, is aware of the enemies of the Church and suffers this burden. But he also knows that the Holy Spirit has called forth many victim lambs to offer sacrifices for the Church in the years leading to the Jubilee Anniversary of Christianity. These are the sacrificial lambs of the resurrected Church. Great will be their merit for the Mystical Body.*

Dear children, please pray as much as possible for the Church because she has many powers that come against her. There are so few who see her True Beauty, the Life she gives to the world! Those of us, who love her, weep to know that she has so many enemies today. But our tears will be turned into joy in the perfect time of the Most Holy Trinity. Pray dear children. I love you. Your Mother

140. **6-17-97**
Love Your Enemies, Forgive Your Persecutors

At Holy Communion, Jesus said: ***Soul of My Cross, I love you. Love your enemies! Pray for your persecutors!** (Jesus was repeating the words of the readings of the Mass today.) He continued: **From the cross I said "Father, forgive them. they know not what they do!"**

Echo My prayer, *Soul! Forgiveness is the hallmark of authentic Christianity! Love is My Commandment! It is My law! It is the Gospel I taught! Without Love there is no life and Love requires forgiveness.

Your enemy is the devil. You are his target because I am in you and you are in Me. The enemy is acting through your persecutors, just as he acted through Mine at Calvary. Just as I prayed for My persecutors, you must pray for yours. Your prayers can set them free from the snares of the enemy and forgiveness will set you free. Forgiveness frees the heart of anger and hatred.

Ah, My beloved, you are thinking, "But what about responsibility!" I say to you, every decision bears its consequence and responsibility. If a soul decides against Love, against God, he suffers all of the consequences brought about from such a decision. And he bears the responsibility of all the suffering, which flowed out onto others, innocent others, as a result of his mov-

ing away from God, an action against Love. The seeds of pain that he sows will come back to him in due season. My justice demands this. It is not for one man to do this to another. It is for Me, the Lord, to reveal to the soul, his guilt, his responsibility, and the consequences. It is for you to forgive, in order to be free of anything that impedes love.

Love is the one necessary thing. When you love the one who hurts you, you are another Me for mankind and your own soul becomes the reflection of My Beauty. When you pray for the ones who hurt you, Living Water washes your soul and renews your spirit, healing your heart. It is an act of the will to forgive and entirely possible through Grace.

Remember that the Innocent One forgave the guilty ones! All men are guilty of sin and must forgive one another, striving always to become like the Innocent One.

*Soul of My Cross, your broken heart exists inside My Heart of Love which cannot harbor unforgiveness. And the Holy Spirit overshadows you to keep you in the Truth of Love's Sacrifice. You are weary and bloody, but you are in the palm of the Eternal Father and precious in His Sight. He holds all victim lambs in the palm of His Almighty Hand and His loving Gaze transfigures you into another holy one. Allow your tears to be dried by Our Holy Mother. You are suffering very much, little one, but the Holy Family of God surrounds you and sustains you in Divine Grace. Your offering is accepted as more precious than pure gold. It purchases for you and the family of man more grace and merit, more love.

You are participating in redemptive suffering. All of you who suffer for the sake of Love, for the sake of My Holy Name, are participating in redemptive suffering. And the hallmark of your authenticity as disciples of Mine, is that you Love your enemies and forgive your persecutors. Forgive as I have forgiven! The law of Love that I impose upon you includes forgiveness. To forgive is to bring peace and joy into your heart while healing the wounds. I love you. Your Jesus

141. **6-17-97 (B)**
The Teachings of His Passion

As Father began the Sorrowful Mysteries of the Rosary, I entered a state of prayer and saw the following:

Agony in the Garden Decade:

I received an image of Jesus bent over the rock in the Garden. Already His agony had progressed to the point that He was sweating blood. O how sorrowful is the Lord! In this image He was not alone. His Holy Mother Mary is praying there beside him. She is the faithful apostle who does not sleep but keeps watch and prays with Him. Though she was not physically present in the Garden with her Son, she was spiritually united to her Son in every way granted by the Father, in the power of the Holy Spirit. Not only did the Angel of Consolation come to Jesus, but also the Mother of Consolation was suffering in union with Him, mystically.

Then Jesus gave me to understand that just as He agonized, prayed, and interceded for the family of man, so too at least one family member must agonize, pray, and intercede for the other members of their families.

Jesus said: **Blessed are you who pray with Me, keep watch with Me, agonize with Me. Bring Me your families. Suffer them unto Me and you will co-redeem with Me. Your prayers and heartache are not in vain. Be willing to drink the chalice with Me…always with Me.**

Decade of the Scourging at the Pillar:

I saw vividly the image of the Holy Face of Jesus as in the Shroud of Turin, majestic and full of love! The image of His Holy Face remained before mine, seemingly inches apart. But in the background, I could see and hear vividly the scene of the Scourging at the Pillar.

I heard the crack of the whip as it cut through His flesh and His deep groans of pain. I saw His Body become a bloody wound, flesh hanging, blood flowing, as the scourging proceeded. All the while I heard Jesus say in rhythm with the crack of the whip: **I love you. I forgive you. I love you. I forgive you. I love you. I forgive you.**

It seemed to me that He was saying these words to the men scourging him. Jesus corrected me and said: **I say these words to**

every man. Sin scourges Me. And all men sin. While the scourging scene was horrific, He placed His Holy Face before me so as to bring His Love and forgiveness to the forefront.

The Crowning with Thorns Decade:

I saw the soldiers treat Jesus with cruelty, malice, and mockery. I watched as they pressed the crown of sharp thorns into His precious Head which bled profusely from each wound. I watched as they draped a purple cloak around Jesus' raw back and shoulders to parade Him before the people. The cruelty of this scene is indescribable. I observed Jesus stand in silence as the crowd mocked and ridiculed His Kingship. I am overcome with sympathy for Jesus. As I observe this scene, His SILENCE in the midst of this astounds!

Then Jesus said to me: ***Soul of My Cross, let it be known that every believer, every follower of Mine will, for the sake of the Gospel, stand in this place of mockery and ridicule. Do not think that in your sophisticated age that this is impossible. Truly I say to you, already, many are suffering severe persecution for the sake of the Gospel of Life, Love, Truth. Many are thirsty for Me and they are denied the sacraments that alleviate thirst. Many cannot practice their faith already.**

You who live in the freedom to practice your faith must pray for those denied freedom. Do not take for granted that your freedom now, will not be tried or persecuted in the future. I remind you, you need not defend yourselves. I will defend My Own against the spirit of the world. Silence under persecution, together with forgiveness, is your protection and strength. Silence is powerful. You will learn this My beloved disciples. In silence you will have wisdom that comes from the Holy Spirit. You who partake in My sufferings, who are mocked and ridiculed for your faith in Me, will partake in My Victory, My Resurrection. When the spirit of the world comes against you, let your defense be a silent prayer of union and confidence. Trust in Me. I will fight for you because you belong to Me.

The Decade of Carrying the Heavy Cross:

I could see this scene unfold on the small, winding street of the Via Dolorosa. I saw Jesus bent over, physically exhausted and struggling with the weight of the cross. O what a terrible sight! The God of the universe carrying the weight of our sins! I saw Simon of Cyrene pulled from the crowd and made to assist Him because Jesus was nearly collapsing. I saw Veronica wipe the sorrowful Face of the Lord. Many jeered at her for doing so. Her loving courage was rewarded by Jesus, who left His Image on the cloth. I saw Our Lady together with the apostle Jesus loved, John. Our Lady was so full of Light in the midst of her union with Jesus' sufferings that her light, seen by Jesus, became part of His Own and somehow strengthened Him. I cannot find the words to describe the union of hearts that I was somehow made to observe between the disciple John and Jesus. I understood that John absorbed everything into his heart, not missing a detail. He watched, he pondered, he prayed, he suffered but he never doubted the Lord.

I saw Mary Magdalene close to Mother Mary and John; her sorrowful heart so full of tender love, was torn into pieces to see Him suffer this much. These people, Simon of Cyrene, Veronica, Mary Magdalene, the disciple John and Mother Mary are the ones that Jesus seemed to point out to me.

Then Jesus said: **Simon of Cyrene represents you who come to Me with small faith, who approach Me with fear, who seek Me half-heartedly and for your sake, not Mine. Take note. I do not send you away. I take your small effort and grant you My Grace. To you I say, "Do not be afraid." Give Me your hand and I will reward you.**

Veronica represents you who step out in faith, who have courage to leave what is safe and comfortable to come to Me, those who have compassion for Me and love Me. I reward you with My Presence. My Image is on your heart. To you I say, "Come close to My Holy Face and see Me. My eyes will tell you of My Love for you."

Mary Magdalene represents every converted sinner on fire with Love. I turn your poverty into richness of True Life. I turn your self-indulgence into self-sacrifice. I turn your pride into humility. I lavish My tender forgiving love upon you. Then you have gratitude and everlasting love, and become willing to sacrifice everything for Me. To you I say, once you were apart from Me, lost in the world, but now that you have come to Me, let us love one another eternally.

John the beloved disciple represents you who are faithful disciples, beginning to end. You who love to draw close to My Sacred Heart, who love to love Me; you who desire to be taught by Wisdom, to soar to the heights of love, who remain faithful in the midst of every trial and difficulty. You are another beloved disciple and great will be your reward.

To you I say, "Behold your Mother." Take her as your own. Allow her to teach you, to guide you to be a most faithful disciple of these trying times. Listen! Ponder! Record everything in your heart. Pray and sacrifice. Spread the Gospel of Love and never cease to proclaim your faith in Me. Then the Light who is in you shall shine in the darkness of your generation. Make your mark on earth for the sake of all mankind. Great will be your reward in heaven. My Vicar, John Paul, is such a disciple.

Mother Mary represents every man, woman and child on earth. Her maternal heart embraces all of creation. Full of the Holy Spirit, she is your beacon in the midst of the darkness. I said to her, "Behold your Son." Since the utterance of these words, her obedient heart has never ceased to behold and cherish, nourish and pray, suffer and intercede on your behalf. Blessed are you who obey My command, "Behold your Mother." Every good and necessary grace will be yours through her Immaculate Heart of Pure Love. There are many levels of discipleship from Simon of Cyrene to Mother Mary. Mary, Most Holy, is the summit of discipleship.

Jesus Dies on the Cross Decade:

I saw Jesus hanging on the cross. He observed all those gathered at the foot of the cross. Then Jesus directed me to look at all the people through His Eyes. I saw that they had one thing in common: except for Mother Mary, all were sinners. And Jesus said: **I suffered and died for love of them. All men sin. I died and rose again to redeem sinners. And I forgive.**

Then I was given an image of a certain soul, portrayed as a leper. I saw that much of his being had been consumed by leprosy. There were holes, flesh eaten away by the disease. Jesus said: **Would you continue to pray for his healing? I died for him. Will you sacrifice for him?**

Then Jesus gave me an image of myself. I observed that I, also, had leprosy, which had left scars on me. But they were healed now. Jesus said: **I did this for you. Will you trust Me to do it for other sinners?**

142. **6-18-97**
Trusting in Divine Action

During the Rosary with Father, I saw myself in a straight jacket sitting in a chair and praying. I understood that the straight jacket symbolized a restriction of movement for me. That is, in the midst of a whirlwind of evil around my family, I remain still, not active in the sense of retaliation against the persecutor; not active in the sense of trying to control my environment or manipulate the situation.

My action is deeply spiritual and consists of a profound interior stillness, a strong confidence in My Triune God. I am trusting not in human action but in Divine action! I believe that God will fight for me and the family! And I believe that my reaction to what is happening is to live the interior disposition of Mother Mary who said: *Let it be done unto me according to Your Word. I must give my own fiat to the Divine Will!*

Then I received an image of my hands with large holes in the palms. I understood that this symbolized union with Jesus on the cross.

Later in the evening, the Holy Spirit reminded me of this image and enlightened me on its deeper meaning. The holes in my hands also indicate that my human hands are empty but the Hand of Almighty God is full of Perfection, Wisdom, and Power to do all things and bring about great good if I but let go and let God.

And the holes in my hands symbolize death of self; a cutting away of my former ways of reacting to suffering. It represents a cutting out of the anger, hostility, revenge, that would have been so natural to me before my spiritual conversion and life of prayer. The emptiness of my own hands is a great reminder of my poverty and imperfection. And the void that is created by the cutting away of self creates a place to be filled by Perfect Love, the Divine Love of the Eternal Three!

Another image was given. There is a type of firework that we have at Fourth of July celebrations, which is nailed to wood, a post or something like it. Then, when a match ignites it, it spins around and around, throwing off sparks of fire and light. Jesus said: **When you allow Love to fix you to the wood (of the cross), you are ignited by the fire of Divine Love and radiate My Light outward, capturing many souls for Me. You throw off sparks of Love for the world.**

143. **6-19-97**
An Enclosed Garden

At Holy Communion I prayed, "Jesus, I love You with all of my heart, soul, and strength. Thank you for the mysterious and wondrous ways that you are working in my soul."

Immediately I received an image of a large plot of land and there were many workers turning over the soil. Jesus and Mary were there. The Lord said: **You are an enclosed garden for Me and I shall reap a plentiful harvest through you. Know, beloved of My Heart, that My Eyes behold the completed beautification of My bride even as My Hand works toward that completion. I am working a wonder in you. I am the Bridegroom of each soul and take great care to beautify My brides. I am with you always and everywhere. I love you. Jesus**

144. **6-23-97** Rosary with Father. My home.
St. Joseph on Family and Mary on "Fiat" to God

At the decade of the Annunciation, I received an image of angelic beings of pure light, myriads of them, assisting souls on earth to give their "fiat" to God, in imitation of Mother Mary at the Annunciation. Many angels were assigned to each soul to facilitate their "fiat." Knowing that an act of surrender to the Will of God would be the greatest good for the person, the angelic beings were intent and joyful.

Mary said: *My children, please call on the angels to assist you in the giving of your fiat to God. Please allow the angels to help you say "yes" to God. Please allow me to help you in your continual surrender to God's Will for your life. Do not be afraid to say, "Let it be done unto me according to your Word." These words are life for your soul. They bring peace.*

At the decade of the Visitation: I was given an image of the visitation scene, Mary and Elizabeth. The focus was placed on St. Elizabeth. As light shone on her image, pregnant with John the Baptist, I was given light to understand the importance of the older generation of women. I was given to understand that they have a very important role to play for this present generation. They are life bearers in their latter life by the power of their prayer and suffering. They can prepare the way for the Lord by living lives of prayer and holiness.

Mary said: *The prayers of the older generation have an important impact on the lives of the younger generation. From one generation to the next, prayer is very powerful. The youth should appreciate the elderly. The elderly should pray for the youth. God's Infinite Love embraces the young and the old and every generation is called to bear life for the sake of the salvation of the world.*

At the decade of the Nativity, I was given an image of the Nativity. The focus was on family, the Holy Family, and every family. The focus came to St. Joseph. I observed his presence to Mother Mary and Baby Jesus as one of tremendous protection, affection, wisdom and service. Somehow I observed in St. Joseph, a forgetfulness of self, a complete focus on Mary and Jesus. He radiated a paternal love and warmth that seemed to fill the cave of the Nativity.

Suddenly, I heard St. Joseph.

"Dear people of God, you are children of the Light. You are created for a relationship of love. You are God's family. Your families are to be a reflection of God's family, Father, Son, and Holy Spirit together with Mary Most Holy. Families are suffering very much. The enemy of every man seeks to divide family members.

"Fathers of families, you are being seduced away from your loved ones by the spirit of the world. Too many families are shattered by the absence of a father. Invoke me to be the spiritual father of your family. Invite my presence in your family and I will be with you by the power of God's Love. I live in His Presence. He permits me to bring His Presence to families in need in a special way. I am the guardian of families and the helper of fathers. I intercede on behalf of the healing of every family. If you invite the Blessed Virgin Mary and I into your families, if you are willing to pray, then Satan's influence will be greatly diminished in your families.

"Do not be discouraged if every member is not willing to pray. If one member is willing to pray for the others, they will draw grace upon the entire family. Be patient with one another. Let nothing divide you. Do not judge one another and harbor no unforgiveness. Sacrifice for the sake of unity in your families because through the family, God's Divine Love is most perfectly reflected. You will sanctify one another if you persevere to love one another. I bless you in the name of the Most Holy Trinity. God is with you. In His Merciful Love for you, He grants grace through the Communion of Saints of which I am the Patriarch. I am (St.) Joseph."

At the Presentation decade, I received an image of the Presentation scene. The focus came on Mother Mary holding the Baby Jesus in her hands, lifting Him up in a gesture of "presenting" Him to God. The more precise focus was on Mary's act of "giving up" to God. Everything in her is an offering to God and His Glory. I am given to see words written all over Mary. A closer look reveals that the words are actually one word written over and over. It is Obedience... Obedience... Obedience.

Quite suddenly, the Infant Jesus being held up by Mary is transfigured into another infant. I watch as Mother Mary turns this infant around several times while presenting him to God. Our Lady said: *This infant represents my beloved priest* (Father). *My maternal arms uphold him and constantly present him to the Most Holy Trinity. By the power of Divine Grace he is being made into a little child so as to exist in the deeper recesses, the sublime richness of Divine Love reserved for my consecrated priests who are willing to surrender like a little child. To the littlest ones, much is given.*

Then I observed Our Lady do the same for me. She presented me as an infant to God. As she held me, I grew to the age of seven. I was reminded that in Holy Scripture the number seven represents "fullness." I understood that the "fullness" of God's Love and Grace is manifested in the littlest ones.

During the decade of Finding Jesus in the Temple, Father offered prayer for a certain soul who had been led away. Mother Mary indicated that she would assist this soul to find Jesus and the way back home again. Her words brought peace.

145. **6-25-97**
New Life for the World

In my prayer room Father heard my confession and we began to pray the Rosary. At the Resurrection decade, I entered a state of prayer and did not hear his meditations.

I received an image of the globe of the world as an egg. I saw it suspended in space at first. Then I observed Jesus hold the egg in the palm of His hand. After a while, He handed it to Mother Mary and she held it in her palm. All of heaven seemed to be watching this egg. Mary whispered: *Life! There is new life inside. Divine Love is creating. God breathes new life for the world.*

At times I would observe Mary lift the egg to her face and kiss it with affection. She said: *This represents new life. The earth will give birth to new life by the power of the Holy Spirit. God's Glory will be made manifest on earth. It will be bathed in new life. The hour has not yet come, but soon.*

My children, you will be a new creation for God. Truth will prevail. The deceiver will reveal himself. He and those who are with him will be banished from the earth. Like a woman in labor, the birthing process will be painful, touching every person. Your decisions now will impact this birthing process for you. I am present to you, dear little children, to implore you to choose life. God is Love and Love is Life. I am present to you to protect you from the fiery darts of the enemy. He entices you away from true life in God. My dear little ones, new life will be yours if you decide for God.

I noted that when Mother Mary would lift up the egg to kiss it, a sword would pierce her Immaculate Heart. It appeared to me that Mary was so focused on new life that she did not focus on the pain of her Heart being pierced. I understood Life and Love beget one another and come at a cost. She is willing always to pay the price, to endure the suffering that brings forth both Life and Love. She said: *I am an example for you.*

After the Rosary, I went out in prayer again. After thirty minutes the image repeated. Jesus became present and taught me. He said: **This little egg represents you, My beloved. I am bringing forth new life in you. My Hand works in secret to form you into a new creation. I am doing something new in you. You cannot perceive it now. Do not resist. Surrender unto Me. How beautiful is new life! You are suffering labor pains. These will pass. New life will be born in and through you. My beloved victim of Love, thank you for allowing Me freedom in you. The Life that I am creating in you will never pass away. Forever we will be one heart. I love you.**

146. 6-25-97 (B)
The Final Marian Jewel

At the decade of the Coronation of Mother Mary, I saw the Coronation scene in heaven. The Crown was missing one jewel. Then I observed the crown come to rest on the globe of the earth to await the placement of the final jewel into it.

I understood the jewel to be the proclamation of the Dogma of Mary's Maternal Mediation, her title as Co-Redemptrix, Mediatrix and Advocate for the people. As the crown got close to the earth, I saw a red dragon breathing fire toward it. And there were many black wolves and dogs barking loudly and persistently from all around the globe. This caused disturbance and delay but it could not impede the Will of God. Eventually, the Holy Father made the dogmatic proclamation and many blessings flowed from it as the jewel was finally placed in the Crown of the Blessed Virgin Mary, Mother of All Nations.

Journal Entry Re: Prayer

I struggle to articulate what is happening to me in prayer but at Father's request, I attempt to record it.

I don't know how I know this but I am certain that I am in the Presence of all three Persons of the Holy Trinity. It seems that

Jesus takes me to the Father by the power of the Holy Spirit. Today, it seemed that my soul was in the middle of the triangle of the Eternal Three. I remember saying, "My Abba Father, permit me to be your little daughter." This utterance was prompted by the Holy Spirit.

In the Presence of my Triune God, it seems that I do nothing. Father, Son, and Holy Spirit do everything. I am so little but so welcomed by God. I think it is the power of the Trinity's Divine Love that overcomes me, draining the strength of my body, placing me into a state that is sleep-like. It is a powerful grace where the Spirit seems to override everything and cause the soul to rise to God. The immediate effects of such prayer are: profound peace of soul, quiet joy, greater clarity and recollection, deep sense of being loved by God, increased capacity to love Him in return, more patience with those around me, a sense of freedom in that I seem to be more "myself", a truer self. This self is permeated by the Truth of its nothingness while at the same time it knows itself to be deeply loved by the Most Holy Trinity.

Journal Entry: Re: Temptations

The past two months have been extremely difficult. The attacks from the devil have increased dramatically. They come from everywhere and from anyone that he can manipulate to cause me to lose my peace, usually those closest to me.

The spirit of harassment attempts to impede my praying and writing. In the past week, the microwave, answer phone, fax machine, and computer printer broke down. I spent a lot of time troubleshooting only to find that they all worked again without need of repair or replacement. The spirit of harassment works in this way to distract.

Much worse are the attacks of anger, discouragement, hostility, futility, doubt, retaliation, disobedience, rebellion, pride, blockage, sadness, impurity. My faith is being tried in every way. Also targeted is my hope. I find myself turning all the anger of a situation inward which results in self-degradation and self-contempt. Father is always reminding me of the falsehood of taking responsibility for someone else's decisions when those decisions are against God's commandments. But the devil never ceases to tempt me to think that anything wrong is my fault.

I battle against these temptations constantly and feel that I am losing ground, going backwards spiritually. I persevere though I feel nothing but pain. But I do so with the help of Father and the prayer community. The Eucharist sustains my strength to "fight the good fight." And while I may feel drained of faith and hope at times, nothing can break the bond of love that I have for God. This amazes me! I love God passionately even while He permits me to be pulverized! I must believe that He will bring Good out of all this suffering! I offer everything up in reparation of sins, but I don't do this joyfully like the saints. I do this with tears in my eyes, anguish in my heart, and a longing for the pain to end. Jesus, help me to grow and to trust in Your Mercy.

147. **6-28-97**
Understand That You Are Loved

At prayer group, in the beginning of the Rosary Our Lady appeared in the center of the prayer circle. She held a writing tablet in one hand and said: *I am here on a mission. First, foremost, you must come to know of God's love for you. You must understand that you are loved infinitely by God. From this all else will flow.*

Then when the Rosary ended, she said: *Dear little children, Love is with you! Thank you for your prayers. Thank you for carrying your crosses with Love. You are blooming in the garden of my heart. As you pray with the Word of God* (Scriptures), *the Word is permeating your hearts. All that you learn now will fortify you in the difficult days to come. You will find yourselves with a deep abiding faith. You will be called to fortify many souls to uphold the faith. You are very precious to God and vital to my peace plan. Persevere in the way of love. You are growing in wisdom and the gifts of the Holy Spirit. Your crosses serve to strengthen you. The cross beautifies your soul as it transfigures you into the image of Our Lord, Jesus. Be at peace. Continue to uphold one another in prayer form the heart.*

This night, I have placed a kiss upon your foreheads because you have consoled my maternal heart by the purity of your prayer, sharing, and love. My maternal kiss is a gift and sign of my motherly affection for each one of you.

Thank you, for allowing me to be your Mother. I love you tenderly and desire to take you to the deepest recesses of my Son's Heart. He alone is your joy and peace. You are receiving abundant graces from heaven. While God's Almighty Hand guides you along the way of holiness, I protect you from the evil one. Though you are tested and tried, you are never harmed. God's Covenant of Love stands and you are his beloved ones. Pray because prayer is the key that opens hearts to God's Love. My maternal blessing I give to you in the Name of the Most Holy Trinity. I love you. Your Mother.

148. **6-29-97**
Formation

Today, the feast of Sts. Peter and Paul, grace is overflowing in my soul and I think that I have surrendered at a deeper level. There is a new and profound certitude that God is in control of everything and that all things work for the good for those who love Him. And the fruit of this deeper surrender is a profound peace of soul, a tranquility of order. It is proper to surrender unto God and when I depend upon Him, I am relieved of so many burdens, set free to soar in the realm of the Spirit. Thank you, Lord!

In the afternoon, while praying the Rosary by myself in my prayer room, Our Lady spoke for the prayer group.

Beware, dear children, of voices from the outside. Trust the Holy Spirit within you. Trust what the Holy Spirit is saying to you as you pray together. You have been guided each step of the way by the Spirit of God. My Son, Jesus, is teaching you important lessons. You have received personal instruction and heard what many others have only hoped to hear.

Your mission is to intercede for the salvation of the world. You are called to the priestly ministry of my Son, Jesus, who now sits at the right hand of the Father in intercession for every person. Your mission will be accomplished through contemplative prayer that leads to union with God. By the power of His Love in you, you will serve the Church by forming more souls in the way of contemplative prayer with openness to the gifts of the Spirit. These gifts are vital to the Mystical Body given for the building up of the community, in faith, hope, and love.

Your formation in the Word of God is strengthening your foundation while uniting you as a group. The spirits of division, pride, fear, confusion, assailed you. But that storm has passed. On the feast of the Sacred Heart of Jesus, Love Himself breathed His Spirit of unity upon you. I am praying that you grow in confidence of the many gifts that are in your midst. Each one brings a unique gift to the group.

Dear children, many cenacles have only hoped and prayed for the gift of a priest to guide them. You have such a priest in your midst. My beloved priest is an assurance of God's favor upon your cenacle. It is a sign of the importance of your mission. This priest has been chosen for you and God's favor rests upon him, filling Him with the Holy Spirit for your sake.

Unity will be preserved by humility. Love will cast out fear. Peace will cast out confusion. Pray for these: unity, love, peace. Lower your voice to hear the Spirit. Trust! You must grow in Trust! Dear children, so many graces have been given to you! Reflect upon these. Then you can grow in awareness and gratitude of your giftedness and recognize God's Presence in your midst.

Do not go ahead of the Spirit. Blessed are you who wait on the Lord. Jesus will direct your path and I will assist you along the way. Learn to embrace the grace of the present moment. Do not worry about tomorrow. Now is the time for you to learn to pray, to grow in self-knowledge, to carry your crosses, to dispose yourselves for more Divine Love. Absorb the Light and illumine the darkness, while serving the Mystical Body. Ponder my words, little children. They are wisdom for you. I am your Mother

149. **6-29-97 (B)**
Sts. Peter and Paul

Today is the feast of Sts. Peter and Paul. While praying the Rosary with Father, I received an image of the risen Jesus holding the globe of the earth up to the Father in heaven; a gesture of presentation and intercession.

Jesus said: **Dear children, My creation, intercede with Me to the Father for the transformation of the world. Pray with Me for the salvation of souls. Like My disciples gathered in the Upper Room, intercede for a New Pentecost.**

On this day of remembrance, look to Peter as an example. He was an ordinary fisherman drawn by extraordinary love to forsake everything for the sake of the Gospel. I poured My strength into his weakness forming him into the rock upon which My Church stands. The Spirit of Love brought courage to enable him to shed his blood for the Church.

I am, today, calling many to be fishers of men, but few respond. I am, today, looking the world over for men to lay down their lives for others, but I find few.

Peter's successor, My Vicar on earth, John Paul, is a true fisher of men. He is a man of courage; My Voice in the world, a light shining in the darkness, worthy of your utmost respect and obedience because his authority comes directly from the Eternal Three.

On this day of remembrance, look to Paul. In him, you see the miracle of conversion! Zeal for My House consumed him. Zeal and perseverance are his hallmarks. I am today, calling you to zeal for souls and perseverance in faith. I am today, searching the world over for men willing to endure hardship for the sake of the Gospel of Love. I find few. I am today, looking for men who are willing to trade the darkness for the Light; men willing to turn from evil and decide for good.

Peter and Paul live! They live in Me! They serve the Mystical Body today as intercessors toward a New Pentecost for the world.

Dearly beloved, if you pray you will have understanding of the messages given to the world today. Prayer will draw light into your soul. You will find answers in prayer. If you become people of prayer, much suffering will be alleviated. Certain purifications of the world can be mitigated by prayer and fasting. Prayer changes things for the good; it is effective! The Father hears the cry of His people and He is moved to have Mercy.

Join in supplication to the Father! Invoke My Holy Name when you pray. Ask! Seek! Knock! Pray together as My dis-

ciples. Gather around Our Holy Mother. Call down a New Pentecost. The Holy Spirit will come and empower you to walk in the footsteps of Peter and Paul. I love you. Jesus

150. **6-30-97**
Isaiah 30:15-18

> Jesus gave this Word from Isaiah 30.
> **For Thus said the Lord God,**
> **The Holy One of Israel;**
> **By waiting and by calm you shall be saved,**
> **In quiet and in trust your strength lies.**
> **But this you did not wish,**
> **"No", you said, "Upon horses we will flee",**
> **until you are left like a flag on the hill.**
> **Yet the Lord is waiting to show you favor,**
> **And He rises to pity you;**
> **For the Lord is a God of justice;**
> **Blessed are all who wait for Him!**

151. **7-3-97**
Faith's Vision

Today is the feast of St. Thomas and Jesus said: **Blessed are those who have not seen and have believed. Blessed are you who have faith and live by it in these trying times. On this day of remembrance of the apostle Thomas, I say to all believers, recognize your blessing in possessing the gift of faith, in believing without seeing, in knowing and loving in the darkness of faith! Faith is your light! And I have said you are the Light of the world. All who believe in Me live in Love to light up the darkness of the world. In Me there is no darkness and you are in Me if you believe.**

When you are doubting like Thomas, turn to Me; seek Me in prayer, in My Church, and I will come to you. My Grace will reveal the Truth and lead you to proclaim the words uttered by

Thomas, "My Lord, My God!" You will find strength in Me and your faith will be reconfirmed because I do not hide Myself, but I come to you that indeed you may believe and see Me.

The eyes of faith see far beyond human vision. If you want to see with faith's vision, keep My precepts, pray, repent, and receive Me in the Sacraments which strengthen you. Then you will see with the eyes of faith and the realm of the Spirit will open to you.

As real as My five Wounds of Love is the reality of your woundedness. Yes, My people, you are in need of healing! Come for healing. Come to the Lord, Your God! Place your woundedness into My Wounds of Love and I will heal you. In Me you are forgiven and made well. If you do not come humbly to Me, you will remain, in the sickness of pride and it will be your demise.

Remember Thomas when your faith is tested. Pray that you may endure trials of faith, always able to see and to say, "My Lord, My God!" I love you. Your Jesus